INQUIRING MINDS

LEARN TO READ AND WRITE

It is important that students bring a certain ragamuffin barefoot irreverence to their studies; they are not here to worship what is known but to question it and inquire into it.

— Jacob Bronowski

175 Hillmount Road
Markham, Ontario
L6C 1Z7

A Rubicon book published in association with Scholastic Canada

www.rubiconpublishing.com

Associate Publisher: Kim Koh
Editorial Director: Amy Land
Art Director: Rebecca Buchanan
Designer: Sherwin Flores

9 10 11 12 13 5 4 3 2 1

ISBN 13: 978-1-55448-606-9
ISBN 10: 1-55448-606-8

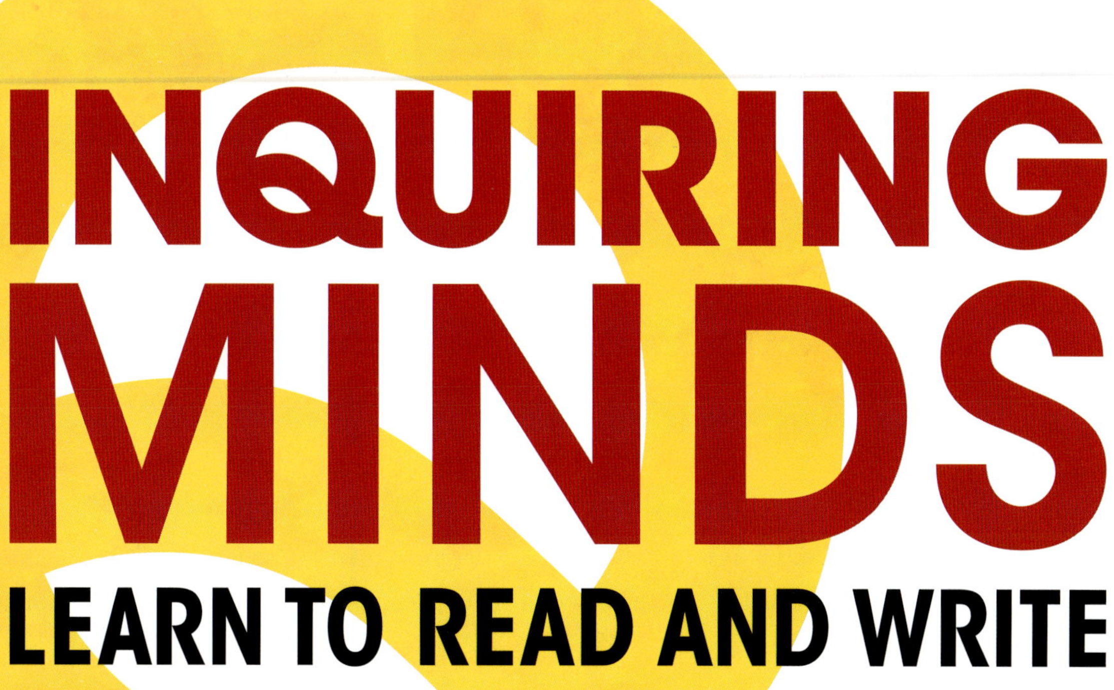

JEFFREY D. WILHELM • PEGGY JO WILHELM • ERIKA BOAS

CONTENTS

Which is the most amazing hockey team of all time?

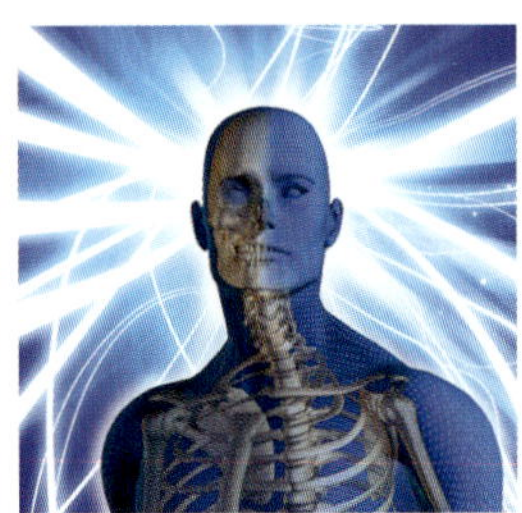

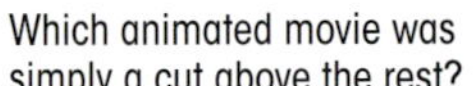

Which animated movie was simply a cut above the rest?

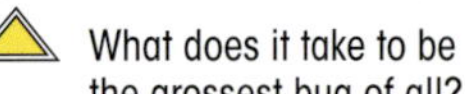

What does it take to be the grossest bug of all?

What makes a building phenomenal?

What do you think is the most fascinating phenomenon in the world?

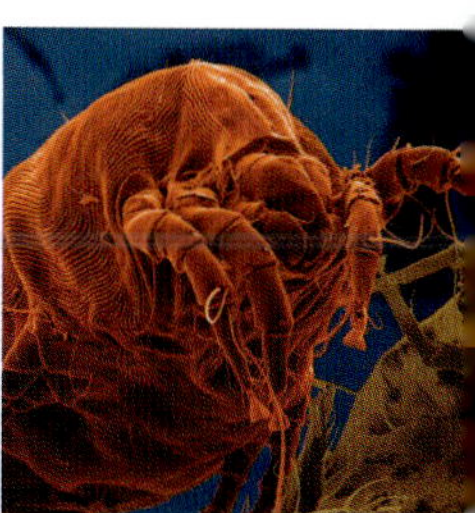

What does it take to be an outstanding elected female leader?

What's the Big Deal?

A rich research base shows it and every teacher knows it. Many students are not engaged by reading, writing, or content area learning. Most students find school to be dull and boring. Students, even those who are successful in school, do not achieve anything similar to what cognitive scientists, literacy researchers, or experts in the disciplines would consider "understanding," i.e., knowledge that is justified and that can be flexibly and creatively used outside of school.

If we are going to help our students to be more literate and to understand subject matter more deeply, then we need to reorient and invigorate instruction. Research in nearly every discipline shows that when we teach curricular topics and learning strategies through inquiry, students become both engaged and more competent as readers, composers, and learners. They do better on standardized tests. They complete more assignments. But most importantly, they achieve understandings that they retain over time, and many other benefits accrue as well.

This book presents a valuable introduction to inquiry and aims at helping teachers implement critical inquiry learning in the classroom. It offers more than 50 literacy and learning strategies that support inquiry-based teaching, complete with planning tools, guidelines, templates, and examples to help teachers design and implement critical inquiry units and lessons in the classroom. The power of the techniques you will learn here is most effective when you begin to adopt, extend, adapt, and invent your own versions of them, in concert with and in response to your own students and their individual needs and in the context of your own inquiries with them into issues that matter to both you and them. In this way, you and your students will all begin to actualize the principles of inquiry-based learning and the endless possibilities of the engaged reader and inquiring mind!

Jeffrey D. Wilhelm • Peggy Jo Wilhelm • Erika Boas

SECTION 1
Introduction to Inquiry

WHAT IS INQUIRY?

Inquiry is all about promoting enthusiasm for reading and writing, for learning, and for life. It is about having what Charles Kettering calls the "tomorrow mind" instead of the "yesterday mind," about seeing possibilities and working for new ways to understand and do things versus leaving well enough alone. Inquiry is about being proactive instead of reactive, about thinking how to make learning vital and powerful by getting after "the heart of the matter" — why this knowledge was constructed and still exists, instead of just delivering curriculum and giving tests.

Unfortunately, inquiry is a term and an idea that is often misused, particularly in schools. Rich Lehrer's work (1993) shows that many teachers who say they use "inquiry" are simply asking kids to "find out" information about an assigned topic that already exists. These students are engaged in topical coverage instead of the conceptual "un-coverage" required by what is known as "topical research" and the active construction of new understandings required by "critical inquiry."

As one participant in a boys' study group (Smith and Wilhelm, 2002) complained, school inquiry is often a fake activity that involves "guessing what the teacher already knows" instead of coming to understand the way experts understand, of coming to know the process of knowledge-making, and of developing the capacity to innovate and create knowledge that one can personally justify according to disciplinary standards. The process of true inquiry inducts students into the business of all content areas, professions, and real-world work. In other words, inquiry is the apprenticeship into true expertise and understanding by doing what experts do.

Inquiry recognizes that engagement and cognition cannot be separated. You have to have one to have the other. Inquiry recognizes that reading means reading about something, and that getting to be a better reader means to be assisted over time to read materials that are challenging, interesting, and that matter.

In our own schools, we see kids carrying backpacks full of books that they are uninterested in reading, and that in many cases they cannot read. This is because the focus in schools is too often on information to be purveyed, not on the learner and what motivates and engages and assists that learner to understand and be more competent. Inquiry focuses on the learner and how that learner learns, but in ways that assist that learner into expertise. Inquiry focuses on the *what* and the *who* of the learner, the *who* of the expert, the *how* of reading and learning, and most of all on the *why* of learning. This rich, multi-sided view of learning is just one reason why this model of teaching is proven, over and over again, to be the most successful way to teach and learn. (See Wilhelm, 2007 for a review of the relevant research.)

The following schema shows how topical research can lead to critical inquiry:

Topical Research — explore and come to understand the known:

Engage with a real disciplinary question

Explore what experts already know and think

Explain and interpret — know the history of how what is known came to be known, see and explicate connections among related ideas, understand and be able to justify why experts think and problem-solve as they do

Critical Inquiry — invent and share the new:

Elaborate and invent — go beyond what is known, see new connections, and fill niches

Extend and apply — create new knowledge and/or applications

Evalute and adapt — reflect on and use what you have learned in new situations, adapting and revising your understandings as you do so

(Adapted from Wilhelm, 2007)

OVERVIEW OF INQUIRY PROCESS

When students engage in inquiry, they are learning a variety of tools including:

» Real purposes of a discipline and how it works in the world

» Conceptual tools for thinking about and with the discipline

» Procedural tools (i.e., strategies) for reading, problem-solving, and doing the discipline

Ask an essential question — set a problem orientation.

Begin with frontloading that connects students to the inquiry by activating what they already know about it. Set personally relevant and disciplinary appropriate purposes.

Provide a supportive instructional sequence to develop and consolidate conceptual and procedural knowledge that can be used as thinking tools.

Read, discuss, question, respond, seek connections and patterns. Keep track of what is learned in order to develop deeper understandings.

Work toward and complete a culminating project that demonstrates mastery of concepts and procedures, represents what has been learned, and makes a case for or proposes a social action.

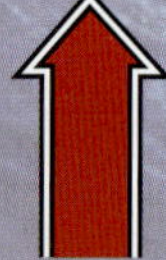

Reflect continually on what has been learned and articulate new questions asked by students that will lead to the possible pursuit of new critical inquiries.

(For fuller discussions of inquiry, inquiry models, and inquiry and design environments, see Wilhelm, 2007; Wilhelm and Friedemann, 1998.)

CRITERIA FOR SUCCESSFUL INQUIRY

In our research on inquiry with teachers from across the country, the inquiry model works successfully when most of the following principles are met:

- [ ] Begin with a problem or issue that is interesting to students and also important in a discipline. The issue is presented as a kind of puzzle to be solved.
- [ ] There is a guided exploration of the issue/topic (through frontloading, reading, instructional activities, etc.).
- [ ] The issue is connected to what students already know, to their personal lives, and to the world.
- [ ] Large group inquiry leads to small group inquiry and/or individual inquiry into more finely grained sub-questions of the issue.
- [ ] Compelling questions are asked at the macro and micro levels (unit level and lesson level, or global level of a text and then the local level of that text).
- [ ] Question topics should be considered from many differing perspectives.
- [ ] Big questions are open ended; answer is unknown (versus guess what the teacher or experts already know).
- [ ] Goals and purposes are clear. What will be understood, achieved, made and/or done as a result of addressing the issue? How does learning about this issue count and matter to us individually and in the world?
- [ ] Work in groups; have a diversity of viewpoints; use complementary perspectives and strengths.
- [ ] Comfortable atmosphere for exploration and risk-taking.
- [ ] Activities and readings can be short, and they interconnect and speak to one another.
- [ ] Open-mindedness/Exploration/Bricolage — active encouragements for students to take risks, try ideas out, make mistakes, and revise thinking.
- [ ] Hypothesize; test hypotheses; justify or revise evolving thought based on experimentation and evidence.
- [ ] Look for definable connections and larger patterns, both explicit and implied.
- [ ] Make and continually correct/update predictions throughout the process.
- [ ] Instructor and instructional materials act as collaborative guides; assistance provided at point of need. Students do their own work and come up with their own answers.
- [ ] Arrive at a conclusion/take a stand about the debatable issue being inquired into.
- [ ] Be able to document and justify your conclusion.
- [ ] Represent what you have learned so it can be shared and used — actualize knowledge in actual accomplishment; could be through talk, presentations, multimedia, writing, etc.
- [ ] Apply your understandings in the world; take appropriate social actions.

TOP 10 REASONS FOR USING INQUIRY

1 Inquiry Provides a Motivating Purpose and Context for Learning

Research in learning shows that purpose drives motivation, determines what one attends to, how one engages, and what one remembers. Without purpose, there is no traction for engagement or learning.

Inquiry foregrounds purpose. Inquiry begins with a question that relates to a central issue and problem-orientation from a particular discipline. Inquiry leads to knowing and understanding something new, and this knowing results in believing, composing, and performing that knowledge in ways that count. In inquiry, the organizing question can be called the guiding question or essential question. The culminating project or projects address the essential question and are made with the new understandings and add additional purpose.

Knowing the purpose of learning means knowing where you are going and why you are learning. It also means that the learner can get continual feedback about progress toward the goals of creating or doing something new.

Inquiry likewise provides a meaningful context for learning. Research in **situated cognition** has demonstrated that the context in which we learn co-produces learning. The context is not optional or ancillary to learning — it is absolutely necessary to it. Whenever we learn a new strategy, it is in the context of reading something meaningful or grappling with an urgent problem or immediate task. Just as a kayaker needs a river to help teach her how to roll and paddle, to provide her with feedback about what works and how, so does a "context of use" work to develop conceptual and strategic understanding and facility. In other words, we read to *do* something, and we develop strategies of reading and problem-solving in service of doing something.

Inquiry is the general context in which all practitioners work. A doctor inquires into what might be the cause of an illness and what might be the most effective treatment. A lawyer inquires into whether a certain action is legal or how to use the law to benefit a client. A contractor inquires into how to build the best possible house on a particular piece of land. The medical case, the legal case, the house to be built — each is a problem to be solved and a context for work that makes the learning purposeful and meaningful.

In a study by Jeffrey Wilhelm and Michael Smith on the literate lives of young men, they found that when boys were most motivated to read, write, and learn, the context of learning met all the conditions of flow experience as described by Csikszentmihalyi (1990). There is "flow" when a learner is so engaged in an activity that nothing else seems to matter.

Notice that the first condition of flow is that the learning is purposeful and leads to meeting concrete goals. One's progress toward these clearly understood goals allows for meaningful feedback to be provided by all learning activities.

Many research reviews have shown that the typical and traditional model of instruction in American schools is information-transmission and that this instructional mode rarely if ever meets any of the conditions of flow. Inquiry, however, necessarily meets all of the conditions, which explains why reframing a reading as inquiry, or even better — curriculum as inquiry — is so motivating for students.

Conditions of Flow Experience

An engaged learner has ...

- a clear purpose, goals, and immediate feedback
- a challenge that requires an appropriate level of skill and assistance to meet the challenge (as needed to be successful)
- a sense of control and developing competence
  - the chance to use one's voice, express opinions, stake one's identity, make meaningful choices, name and see one's growing competence
- a focus on immediate experience
  - the activity is current and relevant; individual is engaged in making things, doing things; there is an immediate function for what is being learned; fun and humour are involved
- many ways of being social
  - There are chances for group work and peer assistance. There is a social purpose, and learners are involved in negotiating and sharing what is learned.
  - There are chances to engage in relationships with peers, teachers, experts, authors, characters, or historical figures.
  - Teachers fulfill the social contract — they need to get to know students, care about them, address their interests, assist them and not give up, and be passionate about the content and about teaching.

Inquiry orientation, as opposed to information-transmission (through lectures, worksheets, and tests that ask students to repeat information), is hands-on and active and requires the learner to construct his or her own understandings in the ways that experts do. Whereas information-transmission focuses solely on the *what* (or the content to be learned), inquiry focuses on the *what* but, more importantly, on the *why* (the purpose of learning both personally and immediately as well as in the future and in the disciplines), the *who* (including both the learner's needs and the experts' standards), the *how* (developing the tools for learning and understanding) as well as the *when* and *where* (the situations in which this learning will be applicable and important).

Socio-cultural psychology (also known as **socioculturalism**) is rooted in the work of the Russian psychologist Lev Vygotsky. Barbara Rogoff and other cognitive scientists in this tradition critique information-driven approaches as being one-sided (focusing solely on content apart from context, purpose, personal and practitioner usefulness, etc.). Inquiry, on the other hand, is multi-sided and attends to all the facets of the complexity of learning in real and organic situations.

Imagine a student learning about probability through a math textbook and worksheets. What if she learned about probability by studying odds and predictions in terms of managerial decisions during a sporting event or in terms of athlete performances and sports scores by reading about The 10 Greatest Sports Dynasties *(from* The 10 *series, Scholastic Canada)? What will change for the student when she has a real context in which to learn and test evolving understandings, and can see real-world situations for using what she has learned (e.g., when she is asked to apply what she has learned to predict the outcome of a particular baseball or hockey game, or a coaching decision in selecting athletes for a particular game)? In this way, students' existing interests and knowledge would be used as a springboard to engaging with and learning the new: in this case, mathematical understandings about probability.*

2 Inquiry Promotes Self-Efficacy in Learners

Self-efficacy, as described by the researcher Bandura (1986), simply means a person's belief in his or her capacity to organize, orchestrate, and execute all the tools needed to complete a task or manage a situation. The research on self-efficacy shows that it is essential to learning. In a review of this research, Pajares (1996) summarizes with the comment: "It is hard to learn anything new while entertaining self-doubt."

Self-Efficacy in Reading

Self-efficacy requires that the reader …

» understands the purpose for the reading
» believes that she possesses the appropriate schema, i.e., the background knowledge of vocabulary, content, and strategies that would allow her to proceed
» recognizes the demands placed on her by the content, complexity, and genre, i.e., structures of the text or data being read, and believes she can adjust her stance to meet these demands
» experiences some initial success using the appropriate strategies to decode, interpret, and make meaning through the reading transaction

Inquiry promotes self-efficacy and flow by …

» being clear about the purpose of all reading — readers know why they are reading, what they are supposed to learn through the reading, and what they are supposed to know, decide, or do after the reading
» activating student background through frontloading, and by building background through social activities and pre-reading techniques so students feel a personal connection to the material material and some possible personal resources and facilities for dealing with it
» providing multiple challenges of varied difficulty — readers and learners can inquire at different depths, go on to read different materials, achieve different levels of understanding, create different kinds of culminating projects, etc.
» assisting students in the context of the inquiry, and reading or activities associated with the inquiry. So assistance in the forms of response prompts, questions, photographs, and multiple modalities for displaying data, graphic organizers, and the like are used to help learners construct and "**placehold**" knowledge and develop new strategies and skills
» identifying and assisting readers at the point of need to recognize various text structures, how they work, and how to read them
» assisting students with **throughlines** during and after the reading to develop specific conceptual and procedural tools through repeated practice of ever increasing complexity
» providing proof positive of learning by helping students to create culminating projects that exemplify, represent, communicate, and apply what has been learned to multiple audiences and situations

Issues Related to Self-Efficacy

Inquiry is an environment that promotes **confidence** because it makes use of students' current interests and capacities through frontloading, and also requires, names, and rewards the development of new competence. Inquiry also allows for choice and **differentiation** because it is about learners reading and doing different things, given their unique interests and strengths, that would still contribute to the common project.

Inquiry also promotes confidence by making use of small group structures like learning groups, literature circles, reciprocal reading groups, paired reading, learning buddies, and collaborative projects. As Vygotsky (1977) proclaimed, "What a child can do in co-operation today, she can do independently tomorrow." Students are always more confident and competent when they are collaborating in a group. Using primary materials and authentic texts helps students to see they are not "doing school" but "doing life" and progressing toward real expertise (they are engaged in the "toolish" instead of the merely "schoolish" (Smith and Wilhelm, 2002; 2006).

Finally, becoming familiar with various strategies, question types, and text structures through repeated practice over time builds confidence. Short segments or activities that provide an immediate payoff, exportable value (something to talk about or apply to the inquiry), and a visible sign of accomplishment help foster confidence. This is why books, such as those in *The 10* series, that make use of short sections, primary materials, and various text structures in a repeated template are helpful in building confidence.

Inquiry promotes **metacognition** by naming the demands of tasks and giving repeated practice, in context, toward the ends of meeting those demands. Metacognition is the "awareness and knowledge of one's mental processes such that one can monitor, regulate, and direct to a desired end" (Harris and Hodges, 1995). Inquiry involves transparency: the purpose and essential question are clear, there is joint productive activity in the form of group problem-solving with the author and others, in terms of purpose setting, **frontloading**, and decomposition of tasks. Problem-solving protocols (known as **heuristics**) and think alouds provide models of how to approach and proceed with upcoming texts and tasks (this is a component of **instructional sequencing** or **layering**). Inquiry makes use of **multiple modalities**, the chance to apply what is learned, and continuous reflection on what is working and not working through exit tickets, criteria setting, review sessions, and the like. All of which work to promote metacognition.

Stamina includes the willingness to begin tasks and the capacity to pace oneself, persevere, organize, and sustain effort through difficulties and over time. Motivation can be considered the continuing impulse to read or learn, and this obviously involves stamina. Inquiry promotes stamina because readings, ideas, and tools that go together are taught together over time. Sections of the reading or inquiry itself can be short but they are part of a larger whole and all parts are interconnected and lead to deeper understanding. Different materials can be read so that the challenge is appropriate and not overwhelming (i.e., in each student's **zone of proximal development**). Assistance is provided as needed. Progress is continually represented and shared. Graphic organizers and other ways of visibly displaying growing understanding, and ongoing self-, peer-, teacher-, or another adult "keeper" assessments all promote stamina. Students are working toward a significant achievement that is embodied in actual accomplishment through a final project of some kind. There are multiple opportunities and modalities for showing one's progress, growing competence, and success.

Finally, there is **independence**, the capacity to transfer and independently recognize the need to apply a strategy, and the ability to use this strategy on one's own in this new situation. Inquiry obviously promotes independence because learners do what is appropriately challenging for them as they achieve new capacities. These capacities are applied independently in a final culminating project

that asks them to demonstrate their mastery of conceptual and procedural tools in a composition or project. Inquiry encourages teachers to pursue throughlines necessary to the inquiry, while still allowing meaningful choice. In inquiry, the focus is on handing over expertise and activity to students.

It's well recognized that most curriculum, in the words of Grant Wiggins, is "a mile wide and an inch deep." A popular joke about accelerated curriculum makes the same point, when a student says: "We learn so fast I forgot everything already." In contrast, inquiry works to master a sense of self-efficacy and true competence that only come over time with deep understanding and use.

Imagine a student who is faced with a long and difficult unit, e.g., about Canadian history or the greatest Canadian political leaders. Many years of political decisions and historical situations need to be studied. He has a textbook to read and no guiding question. But what if that student began by considering ***generative topics*** *like leadership or progress, and what if these topics were then framed as essential questions like "Is Canadian history a history of progress?" or "Who were our greatest political leaders?" He could continue by thinking about what he considered to be the qualities of a great leader, then applying these criteria to rate someone he knew: a principal or hockey coach. He could then apply his criteria to the current political leader. After this frontloading, he proceeds to read about political leaders, using* The 10 Greatest Canadian Political Leaders *(Scholastic Canada) and putting his own criteria in conversation with those of the author and various historians, all the while comparing and contrasting different leaders and how well various criteria are met. This data can be placeheld in a graphic organizer like a semantic feature analysis. All the while, he is helped to develop and name aspects of expert historical thinking which he is making his own. He must recognize his own growing competence and self-efficacy. Finally, a culminating project can be created to express his own opinion about this vital issue: an argument paper about who is the greatest political leader, an extended definition* *of great leadership, or a multimedia display comparing the top three greatest leaders. This project will display the students' own thinking and historical expertise and can be presented to peers and parents at a school learning fair. His competence is proven in actual accomplishment; it is beyond dispute.*

3 Inquiry Provides Assistance at the Point of Need

When students know the purpose of what they are doing (through the use of an essential question and frontloading), and when they know what they will make and do as a result of their learning (the culminating project), they are focused on a few specific throughlines. The frontloading helps students to know what interests and resources they already possess that relate to the inquiry. Students then proceed through the reading and activities that comprise the meat of the inquiry itself (these are known as **gateway activities**, i.e., gateways to deeper understanding and a **transformation of participation**), moving from the ability to participate in doing history or understanding science less like a novice and more like an expert.

As students proceed through these activities, they engage in an instructional sequence, beginning with the repeated step-by-step development of a few new conceptual and strategic tools that are necessary to understanding the generative topic behind the inquiry and to creating a culminating project that stakes a claim and demonstrates a deep understanding regarding the essential question. Throughlines are so named because they are pursued and developed throughout the inquiry. Many other things are learned as the student pursues the inquiry, but instruction is designed so that the student will *definitely* get the repeated practice, in ever more complex and sophisticated forms, to develop mastery of the essential disciplinary concepts and procedures for doing this particular topic.

Because students understand the purpose and what they will make and do as a result of their learning, they understand the progression of the learning sequence, and where they need to end up. When the challenges presented by the increasing complexity of material and tasks in the sequence of throughlines move outside the zone of actual development (ZAD) and into the zone of proximal development (ZPD), then assistance is offered precisely at that point of need, helping the learner meet the challenge and consolidate a new level of expertise.

In *The 10* series, this assistance is offered on every page through pictures and graphs, through question prompts to help students make connections, through multiple short texts and layers of material regarding a central theme, through response activities, and most importantly through the use of graphic organizers to help students keep track of and then analyze the data they have collected throughout their inquiry. If students find the assistance unnecessary, it just becomes another enriching text feature. But if they do need it, it is there to help navigate the current demands and to propel them to greater expertise.

Imagine a student who is navigating a unit on chemical properties. She does not understand the context of use for what she is learning. As she reads through her textbook, she struggles with vocabulary and concepts. She does not understand how to read some of the material, or how to understand the implications. She is ready to give up. But what if this student was pursuing a unit into the question: "What makes a powerful chemical?" What if the unit had been frontloaded by considering how chemicals and chemical reactions are important to cooking and digestion. What if, as she pursued her reading, questions were embedded that connected what she was learning to what she already knew, and all of this to the question about powerful chemicals? What if periodically she was helped to consolidate what she was learning into a template about properties of powerful chemicals so that she could see her progress and have a visible sign of what she had learned as it applied to the question?

4 Inquiry Promotes Relevance and Personal Connections

The primary and prerequisite connection to make for all learners is personal: learners need to see how specific kinds of learning are relevant to them in terms of their pre-existing interests and in terms of functional applications in the "here and now" as well as in the immediate and perhaps far-off future. Without the immediate connection and payoff, motivation and learning will be hard to kick-start, much less to sustain. Motivation, in fact, can be considered the "continuing impulse to learn" and it all starts with an initial impulse which must be a personal one. Therefore, all learning must be introduced and framed in such a way that the learning obviously matters to the learner and in the world. Inquiry achieves this, as does *The 10* series, through the use of essential questions, problem-orientations, and problem-solving tasks and applications. Episodes of learning should motivate more learning as more connections are seen, and new possibilities and avenues of learning become apparent. This is why each book in the series ends with suggestions for agreeing or disagreeing with the author, ideas for further research, etc.

It's important to note that all inquiry is comprised of pattern seeking and connection making. A primary connection is one that links the known to the new. Schema theory demonstrates that we can only learn when we already know something that we can bring to bear and use as a basis for accommodating or assimilating new data into our evolving "schema"— a structured set of patterned understandings around a topic. George Hillocks has famously said that all humane teaching is a cultivation of existing interests to expand these to new interests and a use of current understandings to build new ones — a clear recognition that we must start with learners' current interests and understandings — even if these are misunderstandings.

Pattern seeking and explanation is really the basis of all professional research, practical inquiry, and problem-solving. Inquiry inducts learners into practical research and problem-solving strategies, which is what each book in *The 10* series does as it presents disciplinary ways of thinking about the featured problem of the book.

5 Inquiry Promotes Intratextual, Text-to-Text, and Text-to-World Connections

Students can be helped to see patterns and make various kinds of connections, and inquiry is a powerful context for doing so. It's been long understood that expert readers seek all kinds of connections when they read.

The first kind can be called **intratextual connections**. Texts often directly state and even explain many connections among data or details to the reader. But oftentimes, and this is essentially true and defining of "literary" texts, it is up to the reader to ascertain and make the connections. (Taffy Raphael calls this reading activity "thinking and searching.") If the details to be added together and connected are close together in the text, then readers must find a **simple implied relationship**. If the details are somewhat different and occur far from each other inside the text, then the reader must figure out a **complex implied relationship** (see Wilhelm, Baker, and Dube, 2001; Hillocks, 1988). Seeing and understanding these kinds of relationships are prerequisite to understanding generalizations like main ideas or themes (which are expressed through the relationship of multiple data patterns), and to understanding structural generalizations, i.e., how a text or data set is patterned or structured to imply a particular meaning. In other words, these connection-making capacities are absolutely essential to expert reading that inquires into what various texts mean, and how they can be construed to mean these things. Throughout *The 10* series, questions are used that encourage this intratextual connection making.

A second kind of connection making is called "**text-to-text**." This is absolutely essential to inquiry, as inquirers are required to see patterns across data sets and texts, to compare and contrast multiple perspectives, and to weigh where the preponderance of convincing evidence lies for them. In *The 10* series, each book has a total of 10 examples of the topic that is introduced and readers are encouraged to see connections and patterns across the various "texts," chapters, and special features of the chapters, as well as connections to other texts.

A final kind of connection is known as "**text-to-world**." This kind of connection requires the reader to connect what is being read to real-world applications. *The 10* series works to encourage the use of central concepts, strategies, and principles that can be used to think scientifically, ethically, or mathematically in situations analogous to but also different from those presented in the book. Taffy Raphael identifies question types like "Author and Me" — in which the readers combine what they already know from the world with that offered in the text to make meaning — and "On My Own" — questions that may be stimulated by the text but don't require a reading of the text — to be questions that make use of both textual and world knowledge. "On My Own" questions are typically inquiry questions that arise from engagement with a problem or question.

Imagine a student who is asked to consider trends in the history of music. By starting with favourite songs and recognized trends in current popular music, she can see that she already has interest and knows something of the topic. She could then read about The 10 Most Innovative Bands *or* The 10 Most Revolutionary Songs *and apply the criteria used by musicologists and music historians to consider musical innovation and influence. She could be asked to look for intratextual connections within this one text, but then to read further texts from music websites and magazines to look for points of agreement or disagreement, and other connections, across these texts. Finally, she could be asked to theorize about what constitutes artistic innovation and influence, and apply this to the world by making predictions about the future influence of currently popular songs or bands, and to consider innovation and influence in other arts. In this way, she would be developing and applying a theory of creativity and artistic merit, of appropriation and defamiliarization, among many other things, which would be impossible to understand without explicit help in seeing these kinds of connections.*

6 Inquiry Promotes Real-World Expertise and Application

Disenfranchised students often ask "Why do we have to learn this stuff?" They are really asking about the functional value of what is under study. In current cognitive science, a powerful tool called the "correspondence concept" is used to consider and address this pressing issue. The contention is that in any discipline, the learner is expected to continually proceed toward doing and thinking about the discipline more like experts do. This means that at the end of any activity, reading, or instruction, the learner should have something in her head that more nearly and identifiably approaches what an expert has in hers, or learning and competence have not been achieved (Bereiter, 2004; Nickerson, 1985). If not, students have in fact been led away from expertise, in effect making them stupider.

In inquiry, readers are asked to think about the problems and topics progressively closer to how experts do so. They are asked to "do the toolish thing" versus "the schoolish" (Smith and Wilhelm, 2002; 2006). That is, they are asked to develop and consider applying functional tools that are really used and really count in disciplinary and real-world work, and to forego what only counts in school.

Imagine a student who is asked to study snakes or insects in a natural science or biology class. The student is then asked to rank snakes according to their dangers to humans, or bugs according to their grossness. As she does so, she is asked to consider how real herpetologists or entomologists think about defence mechanisms in the natural world, evolution of particular traits, geographical influences, effects of environmental and human influences, etc. Eventually, the student is asked to theorize about why certain features of snakes or bugs occur, why they occur in certain locations, and what would happen without these adaptations, etc. The student is then asked to apply these understandings to other species or to adaptations human beings might make in face of current challenges to our interests or survival. In this way, students are apprenticed into thinking like biologists and using biological insights across domains. Students could proceed to ask "Who will survive?" in terms of animal and human populations in the face of current and future pressures on these populations.

7 Inquiry Promotes Competence Using the Strategies of Expert Readers

Motivation is necessary to learning and it includes the "continued impulse to learn." This continuing impulse needs to be accompanied by a continued capacity and competence to learn. In other words, as students' motivation to learn is heightened, they must develop new competencies so that they can pursue this learning.

Students engaged in inquiry are helped to read and write more like expert readers and writers through support to do the things all expert readers do every time they read successfully, through activities such as activating background knowledge, making connections, and seeing patterns to make inferences.

In addition, they are likely to also need to develop and use strategies that are specific to the particular text type, to the conventions used in that text, and/or to the discipline essential point: general processes of reading are necessary but insufficient to expert reading of most texts. Text or genre-specific strategies, and conventions or task-specific strategies may be necessary. One of the big problems we have in teaching reading is that we under-articulate what is necessary to good reading.

In each of these domains (general processes of reading, text or task-specific processes of reading, or specific expert strategies of disciplinary learning), developing new and nameable competence is the lynchpin of continued motivation and learning. Competence is essential to truly understanding and pursuing a disciplinary purpose; to understanding, naming, and making one's progress visible; to independent control and use of new strategies and concepts; to future application; to sharing and social work; and to immersion in the work at hand.

Imagine a student who is asked to consider the problem of appreciating and comparing some of the world's greatest love poems. She knows little about poetry, or how to consider issues of quality in literature. But this student is asked to rank her favourite love songs and to tell why she likes each one, and why she considers one superior to another. Her prior experience and competence are foregrounded. Also highlighted is the power of art to express our feelings, to help us to notice and more deeply understand aspects of experience important to us, to consider what we want from relationships and how to be good partners, and how to express ourselves more competently. As she proceeds through comparing and ranking various poems, her familiarity and capacity to use various tools of literary analysis and evaluation are repeatedly practised, named, and used independently. As she grows in competence, she develops independent control and capacity to share and make meaning with others, to enjoy and read love poems, to critique them, and to justify her evaluation and thinking.

8 Inquiry Develops Understanding of Different Genres

In schools, very little attention is given to the demands of reading or writing particular kinds of text structures or genres. Yet this is a primary reason for the Grade 4 and 5 reading slump: students who know general processes of reading and decoding suddenly face new kinds of textual organization and they do not know how to proceed, known as paradigmatic, or non-narrative ways of knowing.

Throughout the first few years of school, students read narrative, i.e., stories. Barbara Hardy has noted that narrative is the primary mode of mind and the typical way we organize and express our experiences and thoughts. But experts use a plethora of particular non-narrative text types to do particular kinds of work, and to organize ideas and express relationships in various ways. Text structures such as exposition, process description, classification, definition, and argument are highly conventional and formally structured, and often very complex.

Every one of these text structures, including narrative, can be more finely distinguished into subgroups. Narrative, for instance, is really a kind of superstructure that can be divided into narratives with a twist or surprise ending, narratives with an unreliable narrator, narratives of mistaken identity, etc. — each of which requires a little something different from the reader. Likewise, arguments can be divided into scientific arguments and humanistic arguments, or arguments of judgement and arguments of policy, each of which presents different challenges. And a narrative can embed descriptions, expositions, arguments, and the like, just as an argument can embed definitions and classifications. This is all to say that text structure is not necessarily very neat, and students will need help recognizing and making meaning with each one. Reading is indeed more complicated than most people think, and it therefore requires that we provide students with lots of assistance to recognize and use various text structures.

In inquiry, learners typically engage with shorter and more pointed texts, and then proceed to longer and more complex ones. Repeated work with each kind of text structure, in context, leads to familiarity and understanding of the text structure and how it works. In *The 10* series, various structures are provided in both short and longer examples.

Imagine a student who was facing a classification scheme for the first time. If she tried to read this structure as a narrative, she would soon shut down. But imagine that classification was introduced in the context of an inquiry about the deadliest or most dangerous sea creatures? Then classifying or dividing creatures into groups based on shared characteristics would begin to make sense. What makes a fish a fish? How have fish evolved in different ways to protect themselves or to hunt? She would be learning to define, differentiate, group, and classify in various ways in service of her inquiry without effort because the context would make it meaningful and assist her to do it. She would now be ready to be introduced to more formal Linnean classification systems used in science and the schemes used in other disciplines to organize and create understanding.

9 Inquiry Develops Deep Understanding of Disciplinary Experts

Study after study shows us that students rarely achieve what cognitive scientists would consider to be "understanding" of the topics studied in school. One problem is that schools try to cover too much, instead of "uncovering" the discipline, coming to use the tools to practise the discipline, and coming to terms with how disciplinary thinking and problem-solving work. Another problem is high-stakes tests that reward factual recall instead of knowledge.

In inquiry, the goal is always to achieve a deep understanding that can be applied and expanded upon. **Understanding** is considered to involve knowing the story behind the story, i.e., knowing why and how experts have come to believe and do what they do. It entails knowing how experts have come to their conclusions, and knowing what other alternatives exist, and why these were rejected. It includes knowing how to apply, perform, expand, define, and offer alternative perspectives to what is understood.

Deep understanding provides levels of competence that involve knowing and doing. This kind of competence is deeply motivating as students come to see the wonder of a topic, the excitement of learning, the power of being inducted into the doing and talking, and collaborating around important problems and issues.

In *The 10* series, for example, students experience specific instances of a topic in each book, and then various layers of that topic, coming to understand the topic and associated issues ever more like an expert does, achieving generative conceptual understandings that can inform future reading and thinking.

Imagine a student who is studying adaptation or design in nature. There are so many concepts and processes to know, from "phyla" to "mammal" and "carnivorous" to processes like defining and classifying. But imagine that the student was inquiring into the smartest adaptations in nature. The important concepts would be learned in a context that linked these ideas to the notion of adaptation. They would come to understand the reasons for adaptations and how these are linked to survival, and different strategies that plants and animals have for adapting to their surroundings and causing their surroundings to adapt to them. They would come to understand more like a biologist and would be able to apply what they were learning across other scientific and human domains where survival and adaptation are issues.

10 Organic Synergy — The Various Aspects of Inquiry Work Together

The final reason is the powerful and captivating synergy that occurs when all of the aspects of inquiry are working together. When cognition is situated, and one issue or idea is always connected to other issues and ideas, then a wonderful symbiosis occurs that leads to deep understanding.

This is because things that go together are best learned together — concepts are important in developing processes that make use of them, and processes deepen our understanding and use of concepts. If things go together and work together, then taking them apart (as often happens in school) will only make them harder to learn.

Different kinds of related knowledge can co-produce and abet each other — particularly if these related kinds of knowledge are pursued as throughlines over time, and given repeated, layered treatment.

Imagine a student who is studying about disease in a health class. What if she inquired into what are the most extraordinary medical conditions? Then the angle of health would merge into and be abetted by biology, physiology, nutrition, medicine, and other fields of knowledge. Learning about the immune system will help her to understand flesh-eating bacteria and this in turn will help her to understand the situation of the bubble boy syndrome. This will help her to think through issues of immunity, health care, nutrition, probability, and much more in terms of her own life. The synergy of the different concepts and ideas and fields of knowledge will enliven each other and lead to deepened understanding of all of them.

Consider how you as a teacher are already meeting the motivational and learning needs of your students. How can inquiry help you to extend the ways you can meet your students' needs?

INQUIRY-BASED TEACHING

Any topic or content area can be presented with an inquiry approach. Here are some questions to have in mind when brainstorming a lesson plan, a learning sequence, or a unit idea.

- How do you highlight the purpose and functional value of what you are teaching?
- How do you actively promote students' sense of self-efficacy, competence, and control?
- How do you help students see personal relevance and connect to what is being learned?
- How do you monitor student progress each day and provide assistance at the point of need?
- How do you assist students to see text-to-text, subject-to-subject, and text-to-world connections?
- How do you help students to apply what they are learning to other situations?
- How do you explicitly and implicitly model, mentor, and monitor student use of expert reading strategies in the context of the unit work?
- How do you encourage and reward risk-taking?
- How do you help students to understand how various genres and text structures work and how to make use of this knowledge as readers and writers?
- How do you support students in thinking and doing things more like a disciplinary expert?
- How do you integrate ideas, disciplines, and strategies?
- How do you make student growth visible and how do you celebrate this growth?

SECTION 2

Planning Tools to Implement Inquiry

PROMOTING INQUIRY

Inquiry is all about promoting enthusiasm for reading and writing, for learning, and for life. But not only should students be learning to inquire, teachers should also continually inquire into their teaching and into their subject as well to improve their practice.

Teacher reflectivity is all about having a tomorrow mind instead of a yesterday mind, and helping students learn to be proactive and forward-thinking in their own learning. To actualize this kind of inquiring mindset, teachers need to provide students with a context of inquiry, tools of inquiry, interesting real-world reading materials, time, choice, and a profound valuing of student identity and risk-taking.

The educational philosopher John Dewey argued that students reach a higher and more expert level of knowing and doing through their interactions with higher levels of consciousness. Thus, a more expert person at a higher level can help someone at a lower level reach something approaching the expert's higher level of consciousness. This process is known as learning-centred teaching, apprenticeship, or induction, through which students are guided into doing what they couldn't yet do on their own.

Dewey also writes about the importance of achieving entry into a community of practice, where the learner learns to do what those who are skilled in that area actually do — so a person learning science should be helped to do the things scientists do; one learning to improve as a reader should be assisted to do the things good readers do. The process of inquiry is in fact a way of making the secret and hidden things that experts know and do visible and available to learners — of explicitly and actively modelling, mentoring, and monitoring students to do these things.

(From *The 10 Greatest Breakthroughs in Space Exploration*)

It is important to monitor that *strategies do not become the end purpose of reading or of inquiry*. Learners and readers don't read a text or inquire into problems to find out the name of a main character or concept, or to put events into sequential order. We read to transact with the ideas of a text — to converse with other consciousnesses to find meaning that confirms or transforms the way we think about the world. Reading and inquiry strategies are the methods to help us do just that. This is one among many reasons why transactional inquiry strategies are so valuable, because they help students to interact with a text and to be participants in making meaning, transforming themselves, contributing to disciplinary conversations, and having influence on the world.

The most significant difference between transmission approaches and more progressive and research-supported participatory approaches to learning (like inquiry) is the role of text or data. In transmission models, the text or data is the curriculum, but in participatory approaches the text is one resource that works in service of students creating meaning and achieving understanding.

In participatory approaches, learners use more texts and a wider variety of textual material from varying perspectives, because the purpose is no longer about recalling particular ideas from the classroom novel or textbook, but about using multiple texts and viewpoints to assimilate data from various perspectives and to develop viewpoints and deep understandings that can be justified and made accountable in terms of disciplinary standards (see Wilhelm, Baker and Dube-Hackett, 2001, for a full discussion of learning theory and teaching).

A highly proficient reader is widely regarded by researchers and tests such as the National Assessment of Educational Progress (NAEP) as one who is able to analyze information from multiple texts and sources and see patterns of meaning across that data. In other words, proficient inquirers are learners and readers who see complex implied relationships across data sets and texts, and justify their conclusions about these patterns by using this data and various interpretive operations. The conclusions reached in this way are powerful generalizations or themes that can be used to think about the disciplines and the world.

In this section, we will look at techniques for framing and organizing curriculum as inquiry at the unit level, and at the lesson level as well. It is important to note that anything you already teach can be contextualized or reframed as inquiry. After all, all knowledge was initially constructed through a process of inquiry. Inquiry is what all disciplines do.

To illustrate each technique, we will use examples from an exemplary inquiry unit on the generative topic of freedom, framed by the question "Can freedom and security be balanced?" The unit was worked on by the collaborative teaching team of Ashley Duke, Josh Hale, Van Norris, Bea Futch, and Melissa Newell. The unit on freedom vs. security was designed to generally explore the issue of freedom in the lives of students, in current events, and in young adult literature such as Lois Lowry's *The Giver* or canonical texts such as George Orwell's *1984*. It took nine weeks to teach, but many significant concepts, strategies, and deep understandings were achieved. We also use examples from books in *The 10* series (Scholastic Canada), high-interest readers that are designed to apprentice students into more expert reading and learning, and can be used to supplement curriculum in every subject area in the classroom.

CREATING A COLLABORATIVE CLASSROOM CULTURE

Good inquiry involves group work. Whether this group is a larger classroom community or within smaller groupings, inquiry involves students conversing with different texts, working on different parts of a project, and interacting on different levels, but all for the purpose of contributing to the classroom project and community. Throughout this book, we place a big emphasis on creating a classroom community and culture that will support the use of inquiry-based learning, instruction methods, and tools in the classroom. Establishing norms and protocols for thinking, discussing, and questioning with the necessary strategies will ensure the success of inquiry-based learning for the class and for individual growth as learners and as people.

Creating a collaborative classroom culture allows students to work together to co-construct meaning. It enables learners to participate in democratic decision making while encouraging them to use inquiry dispositions and strategies such as "think alouds," and metacognitive and co-operative learning strategies. According to Ryan and Cooper (2004), "Cultures, including school cultures, can be good or bad, leading to good human ends or poor ones. A strong, positive [classroom] culture engages the hearts and minds of children, stretching them intellectually, physically, morally, and socially." In addition, socio-cultural theory and much current research (see for example, Smith and Wilhelm, 2002; 2006) reveals that all teaching and learning are relational, and powerful learning involves multiple supporting relationships.

To promote a sense of classroom community and to prepare students for group work, we've found community-building activities to be very helpful at the start of the school year. The following pages contain activities which serve the purpose of getting to know your students and helping your students to get to know one another.

People Bingo

In People Bingo, students aim to find one person in the classroom to fit each category. The first student to fill all squares with names yells "Bingo." This activity encourages students to mingle, find out something new about a classmate, and introduce themselves to others.

FIND SOMEONE IN THE ROOM WHO ...

Doesn't like pizza	Has a cat and a dog	Has a brother or sister	Has a parent/ guardian that owns a hybrid
Prefers water to pop	Has been overseas	Has read the *Lord of the Rings* series	Likes to listen to music while studying
Can roll their tongue	Plays a musical instrument	Has an unusual hobby	Has a fear of spiders
Loves the beach	Knows what they want to be when they are older	Knows a greeting in another language	Can say the alphabet backward

For classes already comfortable with collaborative cultures, you could place a range of ideas or categories in the bingo boxes, such as ideas related to topics you will study in your class. Likewise you could have students complete the boxes with their own questions or ideas. Or you can place frontloading ideas that relate personal experiences to the content of your first unit in these boxes as well. The more objectives and purposes an activity can provide to your students, the more effective it is in the classroom. Creating your own variations on this activity to help frontload and introduce your inquiry project will serve many purposes: creating classroom dialogue, allowing students to socially construct knowledge, tapping into students' background knowledge of your unit, and introducing them to the topic of study. This is the power of inquiry.

Who Are You Brochure

This brochure is constructed to elicit personal information that will help the teacher and the classmates to know one another as a person, student, reader, and writer. Notice that it is also democratic in the way it offers multiple invitations for the students to identify themselves as readers, writers, and learners, and clearly values student identity. It is easy to modify or create your own brochure to meet your content or classroom area needs or interests.

WHO	ARE	YOU?
Do you have any siblings? Pets? Tell me about them. What was your favourite text from elementary school? What made you like it? What is your favourite text now? Why? What is your favourite movie of all time? What's so great about that movie?	Describe your typical day after school. What are your interests? Clubs? Extracurricular activities? What is the last thing you wrote, before this school year? Who is your hero? Why is that person so special to you?	What is the last thing you read? What types of music do you like, and why? What is your favourite song, and why do you like the lyrics? Do you like sports? If so, list your favourites, and why you like them. If not, give your least favourite, and why you don't like it. Do you play any sports or a musical instrument? Want to learn one? Share.

Who's Done It?

The "getting to know you" activity can be extended in various ways and serve many purposes for teacher and students. "Who's done it?" (from teacher Doug Pusey) is not only an excellent example of an initial community building/getting to know you activity but it can also *fulfill multiple purposes.* It serves as a "get to know you" community building activity; a frontloading activity to a new unit; a way to activate student background to assist students in making connections to the material being studied; and a method to help teachers improve their instruction based on what the students have demonstrated that they already know. Obviously, this activity can be revised for use in any content area.

Name ______________________ **Period** ________

In this activity, you will get to know more about your classmates. First, read through the experiences below to see which ones YOU have had. Next, in the class, walk around and ask who has experienced any of the following. Then write the student's first name in the place provided. Do not repeat a student's name. As each student talks about his or her experience, listen carefully and then fill in the answer. Don't worry about filling in all of the answers. Instead be a good listener and an accurate recorder.

EXPERIENCE	STUDENT'S NAME	DETAILS
Has broken a bone		Which one?
Had/has a pet		Type?
Felt an earthquake		How bad?
Experienced high winds		Place?
Saw a wild animal in nature		Type?
Found a fossil		Where?
Plays a musical instrument		Which?
Was close to a lightning strike		Damage?
Speaks a foreign language		Which?
Caught a fish		Type?
Looked through a telescope		Saw what?
Visited a volcano		Where?
Been in a bad storm		Type?
Saw an eclipse or comet		What?
Climbed to the top of a mountain		Which?
Has gone below sea level		Where?
Has swum in a lake		Name?
Went to the tropics or desert		Where?

Animal Associations

Another idea that uses multimodalities to build community in the classroom is for the teacher to give each student a picture of an animal. The students are then asked to introduce themselves and tell how they are like or unlike the animal. Students can even trade cards to get the animals they want. We've found that students are very creative and it helps the teacher and other students to remember names and important facets of each other quickly. Many wonderful animal pictures are available online or in picture books.

For different classes, students could be asked to compare themselves to a character in a book, a piece of artwork, a famous historical figure, mathematical concept, athlete, geographical feature, etc. As with all good inquiry practices, this activity can serve many functions, including community building, frontloading new material, assisting in meaning making, and making personal connections. For example, when studying music history, students can choose a genre of music and discuss how they connect to that genre of music and why. Or they can choose a song that they can relate to, where the lyrics have personal meaning to them, something they would choose as the soundtrack to their life thus far.

Balancing the Boat

It is also important in establishing a supportive classroom culture for students to recognize and appreciate the diverse range of learners in the classroom. Activities that encourage students to name and identify their own strengths and challenges as well as set personal goals for themselves are all part of inquiry learning and creating a positive learning environment. We modified and extended this introductory activity (used by teacher Diane Williams) into a strategy as a means to value diversity and set personal learning goals. Teachers can modify this activity to fit their own units while keeping the idea that every student's abilities are needed in order to "stay afloat!"

Student Introductions

Have the students go around the room and introduce themselves to one another — not as their names, but as something that they consider a "strength."

» Model this first with someone, e.g., "Hi, I am 'thoughtful and reflective' and you are?"
» This continues until all students have had a chance to meet with one another. Then use this as a springboard for discussion.
» What are the different strengths that the students in the class bring to this learning community?
» Why is it important to recognize this diversity?

Creating Diverse Groupings

Introduce the notion of "balancing the boat" when creating table groupings in the classroom. You want to have a diverse range of strengths at a table or in a learning group. If you are always sitting with people who think the same way or have the same strengths as you, you are not challenged to move forward or to justify your viewpoints. Then, as you proceed to change groupings throughout the year, give the students choice but remind them to check, "Is the boat balanced enough for your learning to stay afloat?"

Exploring Challenges and Setting Goals

Once you have spent some time with students, you can use this introductory exercise to explore "challenges." Have the students roam the room once more but this time introduce themselves as "a challenge that they face" or a goal that they want to pursue. Examples are: "I am learning to share with others more" or "I am striving to be more organized."

A key point of personal goal setting is to articulate your goals and then have others help you to follow through with them. This time when they aim to "stay afloat," the students will think about sitting with people who will help them to achieve their goals.

Creating Classroom Norms

Since students work collaboratively in inquiry, it is important to assist them in identifying and practising good group behaviours. In this example, students brainstorm what a good group sounds, looks, and feels like. Then they brainstorm how they can work to manifest these features in their work. Students then make classroom posters detailing the standards they have articulated, and update the posters throughout the year. Below is an example of a student-generated poster.

Group Work Norms

A good group looks like ... a computer.

It is one complete entity, made up of smaller parts, each one indispensable.

Watching our group, spectators would immediately notice smiles and laughter. They would also see an equitable distribution of work. They would see a large number of resources.

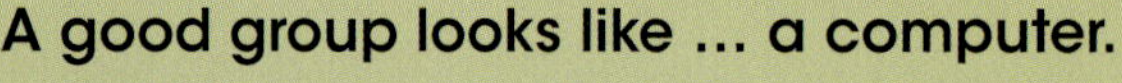

A good group sounds like ... good rock and roll.

It has symphonic sound — the different members each complementing one another.

Eavesdropping on our group would reveal appreciation for individual achievements and accomplishments, ideas for "I wonder if" scenarios, encouragement for rough patches, brainstorming for thinking blocks, and the occasional good-natured barb.

A good group feels like ... a family at Thanksgiving.

Everyone is comfortable talking to one another, and we enjoy one another's company.

Our group is pretty laid-back (see concerns below). We have a good mix of personalities, all of whom seem to enjoy sarcastic humour. There is a feeling of acceptance, which creates a nice comfort level. There is an even distribution of work, which allows members to assist anyone who may need it.

Long-term issues/concerns:

Our major concerns are getting things done and staying organized. We must be sure to communicate well with one another and make sure everyone has a voice.

Think-Pair-Share

Another strategy to establish classroom norms is via the use of the Think-Pair-Share routine. Students think of norms that they would like to see used in the classroom that would promote a safe, fun, and exciting learning environment. They pair up to discuss, confer, and compare, and then share in small groups. As a group, they can then decide on two or three norms to share with the class for the creation of a classroom poster. Some sample norms may include keeping an open mind, listening attentively, showing commitment and mutual respect, having the courage to take risks, and valuing diversity. After a few days using the norms, students can revisit them. Can some norms be grouped together, re-classified, condensed, or minimized? Once a good set of working norms have been established, they can then be typed up and signed by parents and students — as a means of establishing community. The Think-Pair-Share routine can be further used to approach classroom culture questions such as what makes a successful classroom, how can I learn to best manage distractions, how can I pose good questions, and so forth.

In order to foster inquiry-based learning, it is important to establish collaborative structures for discussion and to begin to establish a supportive classroom culture early in the year. The following discussion structures offer ways to do this.

Community Circle

The community circle is about having students sit in a circle in order to maximize opportunities for communication and to promote democratic behaviour. The goal of the community circle is to help the students feel included in the classroom community before working on tasks, and to involve the students in the creation (and continuance) of a positive learning environment. The community circle can be used at the beginning and/or end of a unit of work, the beginning and/or end of a lesson, for reflection time, the introduction to a new idea, or the sharing of appreciations. The community circle can be used to encourage students to "think aloud," using metacognition and co-operative learning strategies. Through this technique, verbal reflection time can also be established. This is all achieved through the seating of students in a circle once the protocols or norms for such an arrangement have been explicitly taught.

Community Circle Ideas

A simple way of first introducing the community circle is to have the students sit in a circle and introduce a talking stick for one person to speak at a time as a way to promote attentive listening. To encourage all students to have an equal share in the conversation, you can give each student two blocks or objects each. When they contribute an idea or question (via think aloud) one of their blocks goes into a box. They need to make two contributions during the think aloud time. Another use for the community circle is to encourage reflection. Students can bring a "headline summary" or a highlighted piece of text to the circle for discussion, or they could be asked to reflect on the day's learning through the use of one of the following metacognition prompts:

- One thing I learned and do not want to forget is …
- One thing I am confused about is …
- The most interesting thing I learned today is …
- The thing that surprised me the most today is …
- As a result of today's class, I will now …
- This reminds me of …
- I want to learn more about …
- One thing I learned today that connected with something I knew before is …
- I liked what Joe said about … and it made me think …

Once the students become familiar with the structures and protocols of the community circle, the students will begin to contribute ideas more openly and freely. The key goal with creating a community of inquiry is to establish the norms that will allow for a collaborative and supportive culture in the classroom. Together with activities in this book aiming to promote and establish norms, we have found the following norms and ideals to be highly useful:

- Listen to the ideas of others
- Take turns to speak, don't interrupt others
- Facilitate the use of "wait time"
- Modify and combine ideas (piggybacking) and acknowledge the ideas of others
- Give reasons for your thoughts
- Have opinions and openly change your mind as thinking develops
- Respect all opinions

An important aspect of the collaborative classroom culture is for students to be agreeing or disagreeing with the ideas expressed, not the person, and to use one another's ideas to think with — this is the essence of community. To help students add more depth to their thinking, it is useful to explicitly teach metacognition prompts for discussions that encourage students to include explanations and support for their thinking. For example:

- I agree with the idea …, because …
- I would respectfully disagree with the statement …, because …
- I wonder what would happen if …
- What if we assumed that … what would follow?

These techniques can be used in classroom discussions as well, where you can remind students that the process for having a true dialogue is similar to the community circle. Once such a discussion protocol is established, the students can be more effective participants in a community of inquiry. Post these protocols throughout the classrooms as a way to not only name good strategies but also build upon these strategies throughout the grades.

Another powerful way to achieve this end is through the use of Socratic seminar (see Strategy 25). A Socratic seminar is a method to try to understand information by creating an in-class dialogue based on a specific text. The participants seek deeper understanding of complex ideas through rigorously thoughtful dialogue, rather than by memorizing bits of information or meeting arbitrary demands for "coverage." For a further discussion of the use of Socratic seminar, refer to Matt Copeland's *Socratic Circles: Fostering Critical and Creative Thinking in Middle and High School*.

SHAPING AN INQUIRY PLAN

There are different models for structuring learning as inquiry but there are key similarities in all the approaches. The following table, adapted from the Tasmanian Department of Education's Learning, Teaching and Assessment Site (LTAG), shows different inquiry planning models. A key feature of all of these models is the structure that they provide teachers for first engaging students into the inquiry, then accessing prior knowledge, building and extending knowledge and understandings, and requiring students to demonstrate and use what they have learned. It really does not matter which model you refer to for planning and/or adapting ideas as long as the key principles for effective inquiry are adhered to.

Comparing Different Inquiry Models

TINA BLYTHE & ASSOCIATES (1996)	KATH MURDOCH (1998)	WIGGINS & McTIGHE (1998)	WILHELM (2007)
Teaching for Understanding Framework	Integrated Inquiry	UBD, The Backward Design Process	Inquiry and Design
» Articulate Throughlines (Overarching Goals) » Identify Generative Topics and Understanding Goals » Work Toward Performances of Understanding › Introductory › Guided › Culminating » Ongoing Assessment	» Tuning In » Finding Out » Sorting Out » Going Further » Making Conclusions » Taking Action	» **Stage 1:** What is worthy and requiring of understanding? » **Stage 2:** What is evidence of understanding? » **Stage 3:** What learning, experience, and teaching promote understanding, interest, and excellence?	» Identify a problem or issue/ask an essential/framing question » Set the task/identify culminating projects and how to get there » Find and become familiar with important data/texts » Develop new data (survey, experiment, etc.) » Select and organize data » Analyze data to see new patterns » Represent what has been learned » Share what has been learned » Solicit feedback » Reflect » Revise » Undertake social actions

Inquiry Unit Template

ESSENTIAL QUESTION:

CONCEPTUAL KNOWLEDGE: (What you want the students to know)	**PROCEDURAL KNOWLEDGE:** (What you want the students to do)

FRONTLOADING ACTIVITY:

SCAFFOLD OF ACTIVITIES: For exploring and practising concepts and leading to capacity to complete culminating project — demonstration of developed understandings

Activities	Connection to Conceptual and Procedural Knowledge	Formative Assessments

CULMINATING PROJECT:

Project Description	Sequence for Achieving and Creating the Project	Summative Assessments

(This template, designed by Peggy Jo Wilhelm, 2006, is followed by a description of each section on page 39.)

Inquiry Sequence for Unit Planning

ESSENTIAL QUESTION

- Articulate an Essential Question that frames the unit as a puzzle or problem to be solved

NAMING CONCEPTUAL AND PROCEDURAL KNOWLEDGE

- Name specifically what you want the students to be able to "KNOW" and "DO" by the end of the unit

WHERE DO I WANT THE STUDENTS TO BE AT THE END OF THE UNIT?

- Identify a culminating project (activity/performance) that requires students to visibly demonstrate their understanding of the developed conceptual and procedural knowledge

SEQUENCE — SCAFFOLD OF ACTIVITIES

Moving students from where they are to where they need to be; moving from their current zone of actual development to a new zone of actual development; from essential question to culminating project. This planning process allows the teacher to work backward from the culminating project as well as forward from the essential question to the culminating project.

- Each activity allows the students to practise as many skills/concepts as possible: concentrated samples, multiple iterations, lots of practice in meaningful situations.
- The activities should work together to Model, Mentor, and Monitor student learning through the use of Multiple Modalities and Measures: Teacher Models, Teacher Does/Students Help, Students Do Together/Teacher Helps, Students Do Independently/Teacher Assesses. This provides practice, gradual release of responsibility, and multiple ways for students to develop and demonstrate learning.

PLANNING ASSESSMENT WITHIN THE UNIT

- Implement continual formative assessment throughout the unit.
- Implement summative assessment of student mastery of the major concepts and strategies.
- Ask how the culminating project demonstrates mastery of the major concepts and strategies the unit was designed to teach.

(Peggy Jo Wilhelm, 2006)

ESSENTIAL QUESTION: *Can Freedom and Security Be Balanced?*

CONCEPTUAL KNOWLEDGE:

1. Students will be able to discuss the question "What is freedom?" by using data, facts, and evidence from history, current events, philosophy, and literature to explore various perspectives on the problem (recall of important data, pattern seeking, data analysis, and argumentation).

2. Students will understand how to explain and defend their own beliefs about democratic values of freedom and security (claim staking, evidence citation, and argumentation).

3. Students will understand cultural and historical issues regarding freedom and security (pattern seeking — how ideas are contextualized, evolve and change, cause and effect relationships, comparison and contrast).

4. Students will understand how place of birth, culture, economics, and the political and social issues of the time will affect a person's level of freedom and security (cause and effect, compare and contrast).

5. Students will develop theories about how to best work toward freedom, fairness, and equality (pattern seeking, extrapolation, theory building, social action).

6. Students will be able to explain how laws and social mores reflect the climate and issues of particular cultures and times (perceive multiple perspectives).

7. Students will be able to articulate what they and others today think about freedom and security as it pertains to their lives, and why they and others hold the attitudes that they do (application) and what could be done to enact beliefs in practical ways (creation and application).

8. Students will independently inquire into a chosen subtopic that supports the Essential Question — Can security and freedom be balanced? (Culminating Project)

PROCEDURAL KNOWLEDGE:

A. Students will analyze the structure and format of informational documents through Directed Reading and Thinking Activities (DRTAs) and Directed Writing Assignments (DWAs).

B. Students will synthesize the content from several sources on a single issue; compare and contrast ideas to demonstrate comprehension.

C. Students will apply and name reading strategies to self-monitor for comprehension (DRTA, SRI, reader response).

D. Students will demonstrate an understanding of text by creating outlines, notes, annotations, charts and/or diagrams (questioning circle, picture mapping) as well as student-framed questions.

E. Students will evaluate the comprehensiveness and validity of evidence in an author's argument (DRTA, culminating project)

F. Students will explain the author's point of view and interpret how this influences the text (critical theory, Questioning the Author [QTA], questioning hierarchy).

G. Students will apply organizational strategies to plan composing activities (culminating project, DWA).

H. Students will use appropriate technology to find information, design, create, and produce original works with supporting details, relevant support, and documented sources that persuade and appeal to different audiences.

I. Students will name and use a variety of questioning strategies (such as Questioning Circle) and will write their own critical inquiry questions.

(Continued)

FRONTLOADING ACTIVITY:

QUICK WRITE ON POLITICAL CARTOONS: This activity will enable students to voice preliminary opinions regarding recent events depicted in cartoons.

Look at the political cartoon and answer these questions:

» What are the ideas or messages that you think the artist is trying to convey about freedom and security?
» Do you think there can be a balance? If so, what is the right balance?
» How much privacy should we give up to gain security?

Brainstorm: Possible costs and dangers of too much freedom, of too much security.

OPINIONNAIRE: Students are presented with pointed questions to determine background knowledge and pre-existing opinions on freedom and security issues.

AUTOBIOGRAPHICAL WRITE: Write about a time when you were not allowed to do something that you really wanted to do. Be sure to describe why you were denied this possibility, and whether you think there was any real justification for denying you this "freedom."

(Continued)

SCAFFOLD OF ACTIVITIES: For exploring and practising concepts and leading to capacity to complete culminating project — demonstration of developed understandings

Activities	Connection to Conceptual and Procedural Knowledge	Formative Assessments and proof of one's learning
Read Text: Using both a Reciprocal Reading and Questioning the Author (QTA) approach, students will read the short text — *The Giver*	CONCEPTS: Giving up and losing freedom STRATEGIES: Reciprocal Reading (predicting, clarifying, questioning, summarizing), Questioning the Author (QTA)	Reciprocal Reading group discussions. Reading Summaries.
Visual Project: Students respond to posted coloured graffiti boards (rotating to each post) placed around the room with whatever comes to mind from reading *The Giver.*	CONCEPTS: The colours and emotions of text as a springboard for discussing freedom. STRATEGIES: Coloured graffiti boards for pre, during, and after reading to help track thinking and organize thinking.	Journal Response. Class Discussion — checklist tracking.
Literature Circle: Assign groups for discussion of *The Giver.*	STRATEGIES: Literature Circle discussion techniques and assigned roles.	Tracking Literature Circle job sheets — written and visual summaries.
Questioning Circle: Students use this technique to explore *The Time Machine* (Graphic Novel) by H. G. Wells and to create a dense question from the graphic novel that pertains to security and freedom.	CONCEPTS: Social and global context of freedom. STRATEGIES: Students use the Questioning Circle strategy to make text-text, text-self and text-world connections and to formulate a dense question for further exploration (link to creating critical inquiry questions for the culminating project)	Small group discussions of key themes of the text in relation to freedom and security. Formulation and discussion of dense questions.
Symbolic Story Representation (SSR)	CONCEPT: Conditions of freedom, equality of freedom STRATEGY: To assist reading comprehension	Class Discussion Journal Entry
Students read the novel *1984.* K-W-H-L Song Lyric Poetry Assignment Guided Thinking Activity (GTA)	CONCEPT: Freedom in society STRATEGY: Boxing	
GTA — Cell Phones Directed Reading Thinking Activity (DRTA) — Reading expository texts of multiple characters.	STRATEGY: Four Corners	K-W-H-L Rubric for assignment — looking for claim, data, and warrant.
Directed Writing Assessment (DWA) — Pro/Con paper — How can freedom and security be balanced? (A focus on school dress codes). Drama Assignment: Students take part in a panel discussion of *1984* from the perspective of multiple characters.	CONCEPTS: Difference of opinion, identifying claims, data, and warrants using PMI heuristic	Self assessment Refer to original opinionnaire completed as a frontloading task to track changes in thinking.

(Continued)

CULMINATING PROJECT: A video argument about where to stand on a freedom vs. security issue		
Project Description	**Sequence for Achieving and Creating the Project**	**Summative Assessments and Proof Positive of Learning**
The culminating project is twofold and relates to the essential question — Can security and freedom be balanced? Writing Project — DWA. Students will be able to demonstrate comprehension of components of an argument. Video — Students will make a video argument framed as a commercial campaigning for one side of an issue that fits the inquiry question. ADDRESSES CONCEPTUAL GOALS: 1, 2, 3, 4, 5, 6, 7, 8 ADDRESSES PROCEDURAL GOALS: A, B, C, D, E, F, G, H, I	In groups of 3 or 4, students select a critical inquiry question which incorporates an area of interest. This question is open ended with multiple perspectives and possible answers. Student groups will select their stance regarding the question and create a video argument to demonstrate their selected position to the rest of the class. POSSIBLE TOPICS: i. Metal detectors ii. Clear backpacks on campus iii. Locker searches iv. Dress codes Students will present their videos to the class (Rubric for assessment). Students will reflect on their presentations. Students will extend findings from video argument into social action. Following completion of their social action project, they will submit a 2-3 page summary, reflecting on the experience.	Writing Project: Teacher assessed based on criteria. Video Project: Student/Teacher assessed based on student/teacher-designed rubric as well as student self-evaluation.

To conceive an educative question requires thought,
To formulate it requires labor,
To pose it, tact.
None of this is mysterious
And all of it is within our reach.

— J.T. Dillon (1983)

Step 1: Essential Question

Inquiry begins when a problem is noticed or highlighted. The best problems for inquiry are those that are associated with a generative topic (Blythe, 1998). Since inquiry tries to more efficiently teach many things through one central thing instead of separately, identifying a generative topic and question about it is of paramount importance. The topic should be engaging, edgy, important, involving debate and multiple perspectives, related to various disciplines, personal and world issues, and should be necessary to doing work in the disciplines and the world. There should also be a variety of appropriate and accessible materials available for students to use, and you should invite the use of technology to explore, find

(From *The 10 Grossest Bugs*)

data, analyze, organize, and represent what is learned. Note that using inquiry increases the generativity of a topic by promoting student interest, connections, and synergy of various aspects of content and process.

The topic should then be reframed into a problem. This problem, in most inquiry models, is then phrased as an essential question (also known variously as a guiding question or big understanding question — though these sometimes carry slightly different emphases, they are essentially the same). This question is phrased for students to be in their language and immediately address their concerns and invite them into engagement with the problem. However, there is a version of the question that is pursued in the disciplines. For example, the question "What does it take to be the grossest bug of all?" is really the entomologist's question: "What are the most amazing insect survival adaptations?"

In the case of our teaching team, their generative topic was "freedom" which they felt was of great importance to their middle-school students. The problem for their students was that many of the freedoms they desired were constrained for their own good or for the good and security of others. The teachers felt that this problem segued nicely with the books *The Giver* and *The Time Machine* that were in their curriculum, (as well as other texts like *1984*) and that the question: Can freedom and security be balanced? would capture what was important to students in their own lives, would highlight what matters most about the two required texts, and was incredibly important in the world given the furor about student locker checks, wiretapping debates, Internet privacy, and many other issues.

An **Essential Question** will be successful if it meets two criteria:

» If it is phrased in such a way to be interesting and compelling to students.

» If it gets after enduring understandings from the discipline/s being studied — whether science, social science, or the arts, or an integration of these.

Identifying A Generative Topic

Brainstorm, preferably with colleagues and/or students:

» What are kids most interested in — what are their burning soapbox topics and concerns? How do these relate to issues in the curriculum?

» What topics in the newspaper — world, national, or local — connect to curricular topics?

» What topics have you taught in the past that energized you and the students the most? What are you most passionate about teaching and having the kids understand?

» What issues are hot in the disciplines? What are the debates and thrusts of research?

» Blythe (1998) suggests that mind maps and webs can be created around these topics to help see how they connect to other curricular topics, world issues, personal issues, important ideas, learning outcomes, etc.

Tips for Generating Questions

1. **Put standards into question forms**

Wiggins and McTighe (1998) critique most standards as being too vague, focusing on the rote learning of information, and as not identifying what constitutes adequate evidence of learning. So the first tip is to put standards into question forms that specifically get at what is deep and important and applicable from the standard.

Examples:

- The standard "Students will be able to identify the three branches of government and the notion of balance of powers" can be phrased as *What is a good government?*
- The standard "Students will understand chemical properties and their effects" can be phrased as *What makes a powerful chemical?*

2. **Consider inquiry and design**

What questions drive the disciplines? What problems inform current research in the field of economics?

Examples:

- How can poverty be best addressed?
- How is wealth best created?
- What does it take to be an outstanding entrepreneur?

3. **Consider the heart of the matter.**

What is the true importance of this curricular topic? Why do I love teaching it? What must students remember and carry away regarding it or we will all have missed the point?

Examples:

- What responsibilities do human beings have to one another?
- How far can we, or should we, go in tampering with nature?
- What are the costs and benefits of technology?
- Is our medical or technological history a history of progress?

4. **Look around the community for issues that intersect with the topic.**

Examples:

- What should our community do about global warming? Waste disposal? Public transportation?

5. **Ask questions about "quality," requiring students to make judgements**

Examples:

- Who was the greatest prime minister?
- What makes a great leader or teammate?
- What was the worst natural disaster?
- The greatest hoax? The greatest military invention? The greatest sports upset?

6. **Ask questions of application. These work especially well in math and science.**

Examples:

- What should we do with what we know about nuclear fission?
- How can we use what we have learned about geometry to design a new school?

7. **Ask ethical questions.**

What should we pursue? What should we do with the knowledge we have?

Examples:

- Should we use cloned meat for our food supply?
- Should we allow wiretapping to protect us against terrorism?

(See Wilhelm, 2007 for more tips and a fuller discussion)

Sample Guiding Questions

Another activity that works well is to brainstorm a list of questions around a generative topic. Then work with colleagues to identify those questions that meet the criteria. You must also find the one question that is the biggest; the others are sub-questions of the big question.

Ecosystems

- How do humans affect their environment?
- What are the ethical concerns arising from the way we use the environment?
- How do organisms interact within ecosystems?
- How can humans preserve unique ecosystems?

Social Justice

- How do we make a fair and just society?
- How do competing values affect ethical decision-making?
- How does a culture determine social justice?

Dance Rituals

- How do rituals reflect diversity?
- How can dance reflect, challenge, and shape the values and understandings of a society?
- Why are ritual dances performed?
- What are the characteristics of ritual dance?
- How can we use design elements to create our own ritual dance?

Artistic Choices

- What kinds of aesthetic choices do artists make and what are the effects?
- How do artists construct and present their works for particular audiences?
- How do ideas of beauty change over time?
- How have artists used the codes and conventions of their art form to describe a sense of place?

On a lesson level, an activity or shorter reading can be framed by a sub-question of the essential question or a problem-orientation related to it. If students understand what question or problem they are pursuing, and how they will be accountable for reporting out and sharing what they have learned, then their engagement will be greater and more focused.

For instance, during the freedom vs. security unit, our teachers created a Directed Reading and Thinking Activity (DRTA) around an article on school dress codes and uniforms. They framed the reading with the question: "To what degree should schools have the right to determine what students wear?" This is a nice sub-question to the essential question, particularly given dress related to gang coding and the like.

When designing essential questions, think about ...

» Have I related the topic to students' past and present experiences?

» Does the topic relate to human issues and human well-being?

» How might I teach so that my students and I work together to build a community of practice?

» Have I made good use of disciplinary concepts used by practitioners?

» How might I explore the emotional, ethical, and human dimensions that relate to the topic?

(Beck and Kosnick 2004)

Step 2: Conceptual and Procedural Knowledge

It is important to name what knowledge students are discovering, exploring, practising, mastering, and using. This is the backbone of every inquiry unit. The conceptual knowledge are the big ideas you want the students to understand and apply to new situations, and the procedural knowledge is what you want students to be able to do in order to understand and use the big ideas. (See Inquiry Unit Example on page 40.) All activities should allow students to explore conceptual tools and practise procedures and strategies related to the inquiry. These are often related to the standards and can be taken from curriculum as well. The beauty of inquiry is that strategies can be learned in the context of almost any topic. Skills should be practised in a variety of ways and through different lenses. Tina Blythe refers to this naming of procedural and conceptual knowledge as "understanding goals." Remember that this is a great opportunity to be authentic and mirror what experts actually do in their disciplinary field.

Step 3: Culminating Project

Backward planning works well in inquiry units: consider where you want the students to end up and then work backward in your planning to consider, step by step, how you will get them to the point where they can create a culminating project with expertise. How will you move them from where they are now to where they need to be to do this kind of work? The bulk of the planning is done before teaching and it makes it easier to tweak activities and the project as you go along since you know where you are going. The backward plan is like a road map. There are many ways to get to the end, but in order to be efficient and effective, you need to have a good idea of where you are heading.

The culminating project refers to the composition, performance, project and/or artifact that require students to implement their understanding of the conceptual knowledge. It must allow the student to transfer his or her knowledge to a new situation. As David Perkins highlights, "Understanding is to think and act flexibly with that you know." Learning is enhanced and remembered when students are able to demonstrate their understanding in a way that is new to them. Typically, we end units with a written composition and with a multimedia and/or social action project. In our teaching, the composition is done individually; the other project is typically done in a small group. The students then have two final ways of demonstrating understanding and these ways use multiple composing modalities.

When designing a culminating project, think about ...

- Does the project allow students to demonstrate their conceptual and procedural understandings?
- Is it authentic by mirroring what "real experts" would do?
- Does it require intellectual quality?
- Does it consider differentiation? Are there different ways to complete the project?
- How does your culminating performance allow students to reach the mentioned standards?

Culminating Project Ideas

Aim to make the project an authentic and meaningful experience for the students.

Formal Writing	Multimedia Compositions	Social Action Projects
» Arguments » Extended definitions » Process descriptions » Classifications » Narrative retellings » Fables » Stories » Picture books » Big books » Brochures » Public service announcements » Pamphlets » Dictionaries/Glossaries » Guides » Newspaper articles » Case studies » Poetry book or cycle » Multigenre research » How-to guides » Travelogues » Design and produce a music CD » Produce an original comic book » Write a children's book » Produce an original cartoon, comic, or graphic novel » Anthology » Themed magazine	» Video documentaries » Hypermedia documentaries » Video how-to guides » Websites » Digital stories » Multimedia personality profiles » Digital scrapbooks » Web quests » Museum exhibits » Museum kiosks » Public service announcements on video or dramatized » Timelines » Video glossaries » Picture dictionaries » Murals » News show/talk show » Dance performance » Computer programs » MTV videos of poems » Multigenre compositions » Public performance: concert, recital, painting, living history museum, fashion show, meeting of minds » Create a podcast » Blog » Photo essay » Digital essay book » Compile and produce a magazine » Create a website » Create an animated film	» Show video documentaries publicly » Host public debate » Volunteer work » Hotline project » Peer Mediation Project » Local Hero celebrations » Lake cleanup project » Park cleanup project » Create and maintain exhibit in local museum » Senior citizen visits/help days » Disseminate the public service announcements » Host or participate in community meetings » Present proposals to school board, city council, service groups » Letter writing campaign » Thank you campaign » Waste free school project » Informational campaigns » Build: repair or rebuild something, e.g., engine, engine model, cabinet » Career research: shadow a police officer, doctor, etc. Compile interviews into manuscript » Physical experience or challenge: learn to scuba dive, run a marathon, lose weight » Organize activities for children, e. g., soccer tournaments » Collect foods for food bank » Open day fair to educate public about an issue » Town hall meeting

(Adapted from Wilhelm, 2007)

Step 4: Scaffolding Activities

The scaffold of activities leads the students from the frontloading activity to the culminating project with the backbone of the unit being the exploration of the conceptual knowledge (big ideas) and the practice of the procedural knowledge (skills and tools related to the standards and getting the inquiry work done). The key to efficacy in the classroom is to know and name the conceptual and procedural knowledge required in each activity that you do, as well as to modify activities to develop more than just one type of knowledge. Therefore, each activity should pack several solid punches! With practice it becomes easier and efficacy is found.

For example: In the Grade 5 class at Foothills School of Arts and Sciences, the unit on Water Conservation began with a frontloading activity to help students think about water and its uses. In the original plan, students were to be presented with water images and to simply respond to what they saw. By adding a T-chart, students could not only respond to these images but also begin to use the scientific method of observing and inferring. On the left side, they wrote what they observed in the pictures and on the right side they wrote what they inferred from the picture. This small change added a deeper level to the activity and allowed it to not only engage the students in the new topic but also start practising the difference of observing and inferring as expert scientists do in their field. Students were then introduced to analysis as they asked what patterns they saw among the data and inferences.

In thinking of scaffolding, activities throughout the unit should allow students to explore the big ideas and practise the skills in a variety of ways. The model on page 52 visually provides the overview of inquiry with an emphasis on the scaffold. The unit begins at the bottom of the scaffold and moves the student to the top of the ladder. Vygotsky's zone of proximal development is shown on the side. The zone of actual development is a student's current capacity. The zone of proximal development is the capacity they can develop through the environmental assistance provided by the activity and the explicit assistance of the teacher. Students will be at different levels but the scaffold allows each of them to work with one another under the guidance of a teacher to explore and move to higher and deeper levels of thinking. Students move through their own particular zones of proximal development (ZPD) to achieve a new zone of actual development (ZAD).

Scaffolding Through Inquiry

ZONE OF PROXIMAL DEVELOPMENT

START (ZAD)

END (NEW ZAD)

MODEL

MENTOR

MONITOR

Culminating Project/Creative Artifact

» Visibly shows how students reflect upon the inquiry project as well as demonstrates their application of the concepts and skills they have practised.

Sequenced Activities

» Exploring conceptual knowledge
» Practising procedural knowledge
» Reading, discussion, activities, continual assessments

Sequenced Activities

» Exploring conceptual knowledge
» Practising procedural knowledge
» Reading, discussion, activities, continual assessments

Sequenced Activities

» Exploring conceptual knowledge
» Practising procedural knowledge
» Reading, discussion, activities, continual assessments

Activate student schema — prior knowledge and interests
Frontloading activity

Set Purposes: Ask Essential Question and Identify Culminating Projects

Exploring Inquiry Question

Where we begin ...

Zone of Actual Development (ZAD)

When designing a scaffolding activity, think about ...

» Does it allow students to explore the big ideas connected or relevant to the essential topic?
» Does it allow students to practise techniques required for disciplinary expertise in a variety of ways?
» Does it assist students to expand their conceptual and strategic repertoire?
» Does it provide for multiple entrance levels?
» Does it provide for multimodal learning?
» Does it provide for differentiation?
» Does it provide for student discovery and meaning making in a social setting?

Step 5: Assessment

According to Lynn F. Stuart in her book *Assessment in Practice,* "Assessment as it is practised in many schools has been like an unfinished puzzle with the pieces scattered about or missing altogether." Inquiry-based learning provides the opportunity to correct this by implementing coherent ongoing and continual assessments. These assessments allow us to get to know our students in new and interesting ways. They also help our students to see how they are progressing toward the ultimate goal of mastering concepts and strategies necessary to creating the culminating project. The beginning point of all learning starts with assessment. In inquiry, we are continually "sitting beside our students," helping them articulate their learning and set goals for what needs to be learned next.

Lorna Earl, in her book *Assessment as Learning,* talks about three types of assessment: assessment of learning, for learning, and as learning. Assessment of learning is summative and is typically done at the end of something. Assessment for learning is analyzing data from students to help inform the next level of teaching. Assessment as learning allows the student to be an active participant in personally monitoring what they are learning.

The key goal in inquiry-based learning is to move toward the greater use of formative and away from summative assessment. Where an assessment is made of student progress at the end of the unit, it should be of an authentic process, i.e., one that mirrors what real experts do in the real world. This serves as a measure of their understanding in an interactive way that involves them, meets their needs as individuals, and is shared in the form of a description and in a way that looks at where the student can improve in the future.

Assessing for Understanding

A major focus in teaching for understanding is obviously making understanding central in the curriculum. This means that even though a student may know the formula for calculating the area of a shape (area = length x width) and understand how this relates to area, length, and width, he or she may not know how to relate this term to the everyday world in figuring out how much paint to buy to cover the area of the walls in the bedroom — in this case it stays as a dry formula not dissimilar to an exercise in rote learning.

If, on the other hand, the student can recognize the formula's application in the everyday world, he or she is demonstrating interpretive skills showing a deeper and meaningful understanding. Learning is enhanced as students demonstrate their understanding in a way that is new to them. This understanding is not graded on a one shot multiple-choice test, but continually assessed along the way. *Real life and real life applications become the test!* For the teacher, it is about providing opportunities for the student to show real understanding. A student may design a situation or think of a way to demonstrate this understanding in a myriad of ways. With any discipline, there are a number of concepts, formulas, or ideas that students are expected to know. These can be based on the knowledge that you are working on in the classroom at the moment. From the knowing are a series of understandings. From these understandings stem what the students are able to do. See the assessment plan in the table on page 54.

Assessment Plan

<table>
<tr><th>Knowing</th><th>Understanding</th><th>Demonstration of Understanding</th></tr>
<tr><td>Area = Length x Width</td><td>Student understands that the area of a square and rectangle is determined by the relationship of its length to its width.</td><td>Student is able to create a mathematics scenario to show how this principle will help solve a real-world problem — student works out the floor space after the new bookshelf arrives.</td></tr>
<tr><td>Verbal irony is when what is said is the opposite or different from what is meant</td><td>Student understands that irony requires us to recognize a literal or expected meaning, and then an implied or alternative meaning that subverts the literal. Student can use the following tip-offs:
» A straightforward warning that we might need to read carefully or that we shouldn't believe everything we read.
» A speaker in the text proclaims a known error, thereby distancing the author from the speaker e.g., "since the sun revolves around the earth …"
» There is a conflict between what a character or characters think and say.
» There is a conflict of belief between characters, or a character believes something we find it hard to justify (e.g., that we should eat babies to solve the population problem).
» There is a clash of style — some information is presented in a different way stylistically.
(from Wayne Booth, Rhetoric of Irony and Michael Smith, Teaching the Interpretation of Irony in Poetry)</td><td>A student reading irony in a text will use the tip-offs and then:
» reject the surface meaning
» decide what is not under dispute and what can therefore be believed
» apply knowledge of the world to generate a reconstructed meaning that makes more sense
» check the reconstructed meaning against his or her knowledge of the world, the author, other books, etc. Ask, does this now make sense?
The student will also have the capacity to use the tip-offs and processes to produce an ironic text in writing.</td></tr>
</table>

When designing assessment, think about …

- » What is the intent of the unit? What is the purpose of this activity?
- » How will the students be showing me what they know?
- » What will I be monitoring or looking for in the students' thinking?
- » How will I track the assessment of my students?
- » How will the students leave this activity thinking about something in a new way or changed in some way?
- » How is this activity layered for all students' learning?
- » How does this activity allow students to practise more than one thing at a time?
- » How will students be demonstrating true understanding — the capacity to flexibly use, extend, transfer, and think about what has been learned?

SECTION 3
Inquiry Strategies to Support Learning

STRATEGIES FOR FRONTLOADING

Frontloading is the most important thing you can do to insure student success. Research suggests that well over half of student comprehension problems can be eliminated if teachers activate background knowledge students already possess prior to reading.

— Jeff Wilhelm

Inquiry approaches to teaching are about providing assistance to students, repeatedly and over time, to do those more expert things they cannot yet do alone but could do with that support, i.e., teaching is assisting students through their zones of proximal development to achieve a new zone of actual development. Inquiry is also about moving students toward the "correspondence concept," i.e., toward real expertise as practised by real experts.

This process requires that explicit and implicit assistance be provided B-D-A — before, during, and after the reading and learning activities. Here, we'll explore what is known as "frontloading" (also known as pre-reading, pre-writing, or pre-learning activities, anticipatory sets, etc.) These techniques can be used to frontload a unit, but can also be used as entrees for particular activities or reading assignments within the unit.

FIGHTING FOR SURVIVAL

Have you ever wondered what it would feel like to experience a natural disaster or a devastating accident? Can you imagine what goes through the minds of victims as they are sucked up by a tornado or washed away in a giant wave? What about those who are attacked by vicious animals, such as sharks or swarms of killer bees?

People who survive experiences like these have some terrifying stories to tell! Their experiences affect them physically and mentally and often haunt them for the rest of their lives.

(From *The 10 Most Terrifying Experiences*)

Write On!

Have you ever read a book that you couldn't put down till the end? Or a poem with which you really connected? If so, you have been fortunate enough to find the magic in words. As writer Alberto Manguel wrote, "Words, the squiggles that dance before our eyes on the page and the sounds they create in the darkness of the mind, are essentially a form of magic. From literally thin air, the words the writer puts down allow us to discover, capture, explore, identify, transform, analyze, and ultimately inhabit the world around and within us. And sometimes almost understand it." Throughout history, there have been many amazing and accomplished writers who have created this magic for their readers with their poetry, plays, novels, and short stories. Their imaginative and brilliant works have touched and inspired readers around the world.

In this book, we present our choice of the 10 most remarkable writers. We selected and ranked them using these criteria: The extent to which their writings have touched and inspired readers; their talent at writing; their influence on other writers; the length of time that their works have endured; the number of copies their books have sold — around the world and in different languages; and the awards that they have won.

(From *The 10 Most Remarkable Writers*)

Frontloading is what you do before the reading and learning activities to:

- create interest
- foreground purpose
- activate background knowledge the students already possess
- build background that they do not possess but will need in order to be successful with the current task (this is often achieved naturally as some students know things that others do not, thus building the group's prior knowledge)
- provide some kind of response template to assist in constructing and placeholding emergent understandings over the course of the unit

When designing frontloading activities, think about ...

- How does your activity activate and build the students' prior knowledge or background information regarding your unit inquiry?
- How does the activity work to motivate students for reading and inquiry regarding the theme?
- How will the frontloading activity work to organize inquiry, set purposes, and consolidate learning about the theme throughout the unit, i.e., how will it help students set purposes for their reading, focus their learning, clarify what they are coming to know, and help them to monitor their learning progress?

Autobiographical Writing

Research by Brian White (1995) shows that the strategy of autobiographical writing, which enables students to personally relate and bring personal relevance to the learning, hugely increases engagement and comprehension in subsequent reading and learning. Simply have students write autobiographically in a way that is related to the topic. For example, from the freedom vs. security unit: Write about a time when you were not allowed to do something that you really wanted to do. Be sure to describe why you were denied this possibility, and whether you think there was any real justification for denying you this "freedom." Point out that many famous writers and poets write autobiographically. A good example is Emily Dickinson, one of the most original minds in the history of English literature.

An oil painting of Emily Dickinson as a child

During her lifetime, the quiet Emily Dickinson from Amherst, Massachusetts, kept much of her poetry hidden. After her death, she came to be regarded as one of the most original geniuses in the history of English literature. Here is one of her original poems.

"I'm nobody! Who are you?"

I'm nobody! Who are you?
Are you nobody, too?
Then there's a pair of us – don't tell!
They'd banish us, you know.

How dreary to be somebody!
How public, like a frog
To tell your name the livelong day
To an admiring bog!

(From *The 10 Most Remarkable Writers*)

Brainstorming

In a brainstorming session, students are asked to quickly list answers to a prompt or prompts related to the inquiry. They then share their lists with a small group and later share with the whole class to make a master list. These lists can be added to, amended, and used in various ways throughout the unit.

To prime the pump, you might provide an example or two before students write, or you might ask for a couple of ideas from the class. The brainstorming should move quickly. This activates student background and promotes personal connection making. The sharing builds background knowledge since students will have different ideas. Here is an example of brainstorming prompts for the freedom and security unit.

Example: Freedom to/freedom from

Possible costs and dangers:

» *Take a couple of minutes to list the most important things you want freedom to do ... these can be things you want to do right now or in the future.*

For example, I want the freedom of education — I want to be able to go to university without amassing huge amounts of debt.

» *Next, list what might keep you from doing these things ...*

So, for my example, the current and traditional system of open admissions and tuition at universities might keep me from this freedom.

» *Here's a different take on freedom. What do you want freedom from?*

For example, I would like freedom from the fear of getting blown up when I fly in an airplane.

» *Last, list what might provide us with freedom from those issues?*

In my example, this freedom is provided by airport security personnel and airport rules and regulations.

In a follow-up discussion, it can be pointed out that we desire a lot of freedoms but we often have to give up something to get them. For example, we give up some of our rights to privacy for what we consider the greater freedom of not worrying about being victims of hijacking and terrorism when we fly.

Types of freedom with the cause and effect can be tracked through anchor charts throughout the unit, allowing students to make adaptations and deletions as they gain more understanding.

STRATEGY 3

See, Think, Wonder

Another way to engage students into thinking about a new inquiry unit is to use the See, Think, Wonder strategy. As a frontloading task to a critical literacy unit on advertising, a teacher presented her students with the following image and then led the class into a discussion with "What do you see?" "What are you thinking?" and "What are you wondering about?"

(A public service announcement from The Skin Cancer Foundation)

See, Think, Wonder		
What do you see?	**What are you thinking?**	**What are you wondering about?**
A woman lying on the beach	She has no cares in the world.	Does she realize that she is being watched?
People in mourning	They are dressed in black to contrast with the girl in the swimsuit.	Why are they on the beach?
Blue skies and a sunny outlook	Is this an advertisement for sun protection products or a message about skin cancer?	If this is an advertisement for skin cancer awareness, why has the advertiser presented this image to us?

(A public service announcement from the Canadian Hockey Association)

Three-Level Questioning Guide

On the lines:

» What is the image of?
» What is in the image?

Between the lines:

» Who is the advertiser targeting? (Target audience)
» What benefit/lifestyle is the advertisement promoting?
» What is being sold/ promoted?
» What is the message?

Beyond the lines:

» What is the purpose of advertising?
» In what ways are advertisers responsible for their campaigns and the effects of their ads?

(Also see Strategy 26 on page 98.)

The See, Think, Wonder strategy creates a solid foundation on which to sequence other activities. This strategy was used with Grade 7 students at New Norfolk High School in Tasmania. The students were told about the advertiser further into the unit. They learned about the different techniques used by advertisers and they revisited the advertisements presented in class. One group of students wrote a series of three-level questions, using a three-level questioning guide as a way to critically examine advertisements. The See, Think, Wonder strategy is adaptable for any unit as well as activity to allow students to tap into their own knowledge and see new connections.

STRATEGY 4

K-W-H-L

The K-W-H-L strategy allows a teacher to find out what the students already know so as to make his or her overall teaching more effective. Through this strategy, teachers can be better aware of gaps in learning or perhaps even be alerted to a learning problem. The curriculum becomes more focused and has greater impact on weak areas. The chart should remain on display in the classroom and be regularly used as a reference, as well as the place where additional information can be posted. Students will soon learn to see real-world applications of this technique and use it effectively for research, preparation, and instruction. Students will learn to challenge themselves through effective goal setting and learn to reap the benefits in their own learning and growth as their ability to problem solve increases and their confidence is developed.

K-W-H-L works because students activate what they already know (K) and build on this (as different students share different information), set purposes (W), make a plan for pursuing these purposes (H), and have a template for recording what has been learned (L). All of the criteria of good frontloading are met!

K	W	H	L
What I Know	**What I Want to Know or What I Want to Solve**	**How Will I Find Information** (Which resources, websites, texts, formulas, methods, etc.)	**What I Learned**

Example: Freedom, Security, and Censorship

What I Know	What I Want to Know	How Will I Find Information	What I Learned
Definition: Deciding what others should read, see, or know is censorship. Widely practised during the Cold War both in the USSR and United States. Nazi Germany burned books to control the people's ideas. It is dangerous. It is a means of control. It can be good if it protects children or others from hate crimes, etc. Internet filters at school and home are a form of censorship. Our school newspaper is censored because there are things we can't write about. Censorship can be done in many ways. It gives power to those who are in control of information. Controls what we think because it controls what we know. Often used with pornography and violence to "protect" us from these controls.	Is censorship legal? Does it still go on today in Canada? In other countries? If so, should we have it at all? If not, should we start it? Is censorship brainwashing? Is it a tool of totalitarian governments? How? Who does censorship today? Where and on what? How does censorship affect personal freedom? Can freedom exist with censorship? How does censorship affect politics and vice versa? Is censorship moral? What is the difference between censorship and just making some choices for others? Can we protect children until they are able to handle unsavoury ideas? Is it our duty and responsibility as a culture to protect children into adulthood? Can this actually be done?	Encyclopedias Websites Novels Historical journals Political periodicals Museums Civil Rights/Human Rights Museum Library resources: CD-ROMs, reference tools, newspapers Media	Restraint on publication is unconstitutional and only a few exceptional circumstances may justify a restraint. Censorship happens today even in Canada. Censorship is a tool of totalitarian regimes to obtain control over the thoughts, beliefs, and actions of a group. The government can censor information during wartime to protect the missions. They can also classify information related to national security. Schools also practise censorship in legal ways because they act *in loco parentis* (Latin for "in place of a parent"). Censorship involves issues of federal vs. individual rights. It is becoming more of an issue with the Web and MP3 files.

Opinionnaires and Rankings

There are a plethora of other more sophisticated frontloading techniques such as rankings, surveys, and analogy organizers that compare what kids know about to what they don't know about, such as role plays, drama situations, and much more (see Wilhelm, et al, 2001). On the next page is an example of an opinionnaire used for the freedom vs. security unit. Opinionnaires are excellent frontloading devices because students are required to make and justify decisions regarding the inquiry. This requires activating their background beliefs and experiences. They can return to the opinionnaire throughout the unit to discuss the responses of various characters, authors, or experts. As they do, they are practising making inferences, seeing connections, justifying conclusions, and creating mini-arguments using data and interpretive warrants — all necessary to develop informed positions and afford true understanding. Students can also return to the survey after the unit to see how and why their own initial opinions may have been deepened, evolved, or changed.

Sample Opinionnaire: CAN FREEDOM AND SECURITY BE BALANCED?

These questions must be answered with either a Yes or a No. No exceptions. Be prepared to justify your answers.

STATEMENTS:	YES	NO
I am willing to give up my right to privacy if it means the government can catch the bad guys.		
It is worth working more than 40 hours a week to feel financially secure.		
I am happy to pay 35% of all I earn for protection and security from the police, fire department, armed forces, etc.		
National security must always supersede citizens' rights.		
It is wrong for the government to tap phone lines or control Internet use.		
Laws restricting possibly dangerous activities (cliff diving, swimming, rafting) on public land are violations of our freedom and are unnecessary.		
Being searched or going through metal detectors before entering school is okay.		
Profiling, or searching people because they are of a certain ethnicity or religious group, is stereotyping and is wrong. It should never be done.		
If we allow illegal immigrants equal civil liberties we will be subject to more crime and our security will be jeopardized.		

Now split up into groups of four or five and discuss these questions while remaining completely true to your answer. Focus on those questions on which your group disagrees. Do not be wishy-washy. There are no grey areas here. You will report out on one of the comments on which your group most strongly disagreed, explaining the reasons for your disagreement.

After this is done, begin a full class discussion on the findings and why the activity was difficult. This would help to lead into the generative understanding regarding the difficulties of balancing security and freedom, and the emotional, political, and ethical issues that are implicated.

STRATEGY 6

Where Do I Stand?

Another useful frontloading activity that aims to tune students into the inquiry and tap into existing knowledge and viewpoints toward a certain topical concept or idea is "Where Do I Stand?" The students are given a topical statement or a question, such as, "The world would be better off without censorship." The students can then be asked to position themselves on an imaginary line in the classroom. At one end is strongly agree, then agree, standing in the middle, then disagree, and on the opposite end — strongly disagree. Once positioned, the students need to justify where they stand using what they already know. The line can then be folded in half so that all students stand opposite a partner. The most strongly agreed person will now stand opposite the strongly disagree person. This makes for an interesting sharing of ideas and discussion. This "on the line challenge," often referred to as "Where Do I Stand?" is a great way to also begin a think/pair/share. The students can revisit this idea at the end of a lesson or learning sequence to see how their views have changed and/or deepened.

Four Corners

This is a variation of the "Where Do I Stand?" strategy. Students can walk to a corner designated as "strongly agree," "agree," "disagree," or "strongly disagree" as their response to a statement. They can confer with those in their corner to make a statement or manifesto of why they stand where they do. Or they could pair up with students from another corner to discuss their views. Designate each classroom corner as an answer to a controversial scenario. Students choose an answer by selecting the corner that corresponds to the solution that resonates best with them. Then they discuss their reasoning with others.

Corner 1: Agree	Corner 2: Strongly Agree
Corner 3: Disagree	**Corner 4:** Strongly Disagree

Example: Cell phone use in schools

Corner 1: There are to be no cell phones allowed in school. On sight, they will be taken from the student and placed in the main office for collection by a parent.

Corner 2: Cell phones can only be used during lunchtime, before school, and after school.

Corner 3: Cell phones can be brought to class and used for emergency situations but should be kept in silent mode and should not distract from the learning process.

Corner 4: Cell phones can be brought to school. Students should be excused from class to answer the phone call if they have a reason to do so.

Note: This example can be used to tie in with the exemplar unit of "Can freedom and security be balanced?"

STRATEGY 8

Mind Mapping

Mind Mapping is also referred to as concept mapping. Both share the same common principles: the idea of writing down a central idea or concept and then thinking up new and related ideas which branch out from the centre. We find the mind map to be a useful frontloading exercise for inquiry when the essential question or a guiding question is placed in the centre. The students first write down initial thoughts and ideas (allowing the teacher to gauge what is known) and then as more context is provided for the students, they can begin to connect new knowledge to existing knowledge.

Here is an example, using the question, "What does it take to be a good leader?" The students are asked a question. Then they write down their initial thoughts. These are arranged in the mind map. A way of structuring the mind map is to ask the students to colour-code their responses or use symbols or graphics. As they begin to make connections, further questions are raised (shown here in red) and a good idea is to have the students ground their thinking with personal connections (shown here in green). As the students uncover more about the concept, topic, or question, they build onto their mind maps and therefore their understanding. This activity begins as a frontloading activity but then can be used as a way for students and the teacher to visibly track the student's thinking throughout the unit.

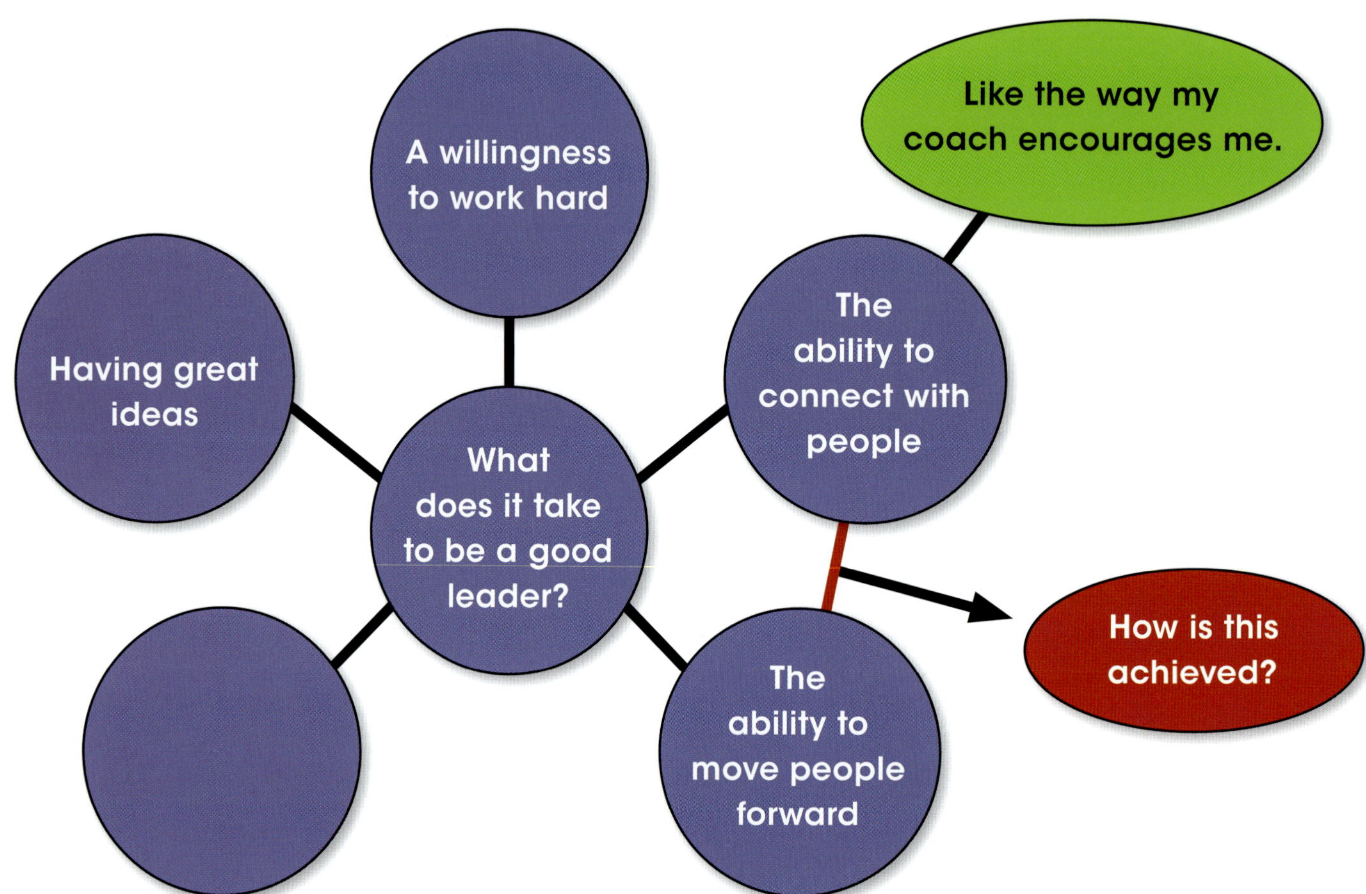

Frayer Model

The Frayer model was created by Dorothy A. Frayer and associates. It may be used as a frontloading activity to a unit or activity, as a way to organize thought throughout a unit plan, or as a way to define vocabulary. We keep these models on wall charts and students add or delete information to each square after their activities throughout the unit. The centre oval is used for an essential question such as: What is a polygon? (See example below.) Other questions could be: What are civil rights? What is a community? Who is a hero? What is true innovation?

DEFINITION	CHARACTERISTICS
» A mathematical shape that is a closed plane figure bounded by three or more line segments	» Closed plane figure » More than two straight lines » Two-dimensional » Made of line segments
What is a polygon?	
EXAMPLES	**NON-EXAMPLES**
» Pentagon » Hexagon » Square » Trapezoid » Rhombus	» Circle » Cone » Arrow » Cylinder

(From Frayer, D.A., W. D. Frederick, and H. J. Klausmeier, 1969, "A schema for testing the level of concept mastery" (working paper No. 16), Madison: Wisconsin Research and Development Center for Cognitive Learning.)

STRATEGIES FOR READING AND THINK ALOUD

Good frontloading does a tremendous amount of work to help students to activate personal knowledge and then to have this available to connect to the texts and data they will study. It is important to keep encouraging this kind of connection making throughout the unit, and to promote other connections like text-to-text (intertextual) or data set to data set connections, and connections from what is learned to the world and possible future applications. Understanding requires connecting oneself to the material, and connecting the material back to the world and its use. This is one reason why inquiry so powerfully fosters understanding. Inquiry is about pattern seeking and connecting the dots so knowledge can be justified with the "story behind the story."

This section focuses on reading strategies that can assist in the guided learning/ scaffolding of learning. We will show how to do so using the questioning circle, and how to use group structures such as reciprocal reading or literature circle roles with embedded assistance specifically for seeing and making such connections, and finally how to use a guided reading assignment with a response template for doing so.

As teachers we need to explicitly model and teach what good readers and problem-solvers do. As we gradually release the responsibility for meaning making onto our students, it is first important to explicitly model a strategy and then apprentice our students to use the strategy, and to scaffold the learning and direct the students toward independent use.

The Questioning Circle

The Questioning Circle (Kelly and Christenbury, 1983) is for use with longer segments of text, and questioning circles can also be designed to consider and reflect upon a whole unit (see Wilhelm, 2007). The questioning circle provides a structured framework for developing questions about a text. The strategy helps teachers to devise questions that are interesting and engaging to students — it helps students to think more critically about a text and to see how the text connects personally to their own lives. The questioning circle consists of three overlapping areas of knowledge that expert readers bring to bear when reading:

Knowledge of the text being read → **TEXT**
Personal knowledge and experience → **READER**
Knowledge of the world and other texts → **WORLD**

As the following diagram shows, the three areas overlap and create a central dense area. The dense centre represents the highest-order thinking about a text. It contains more complex questions that require using all three resources: the personal, textual, and world.

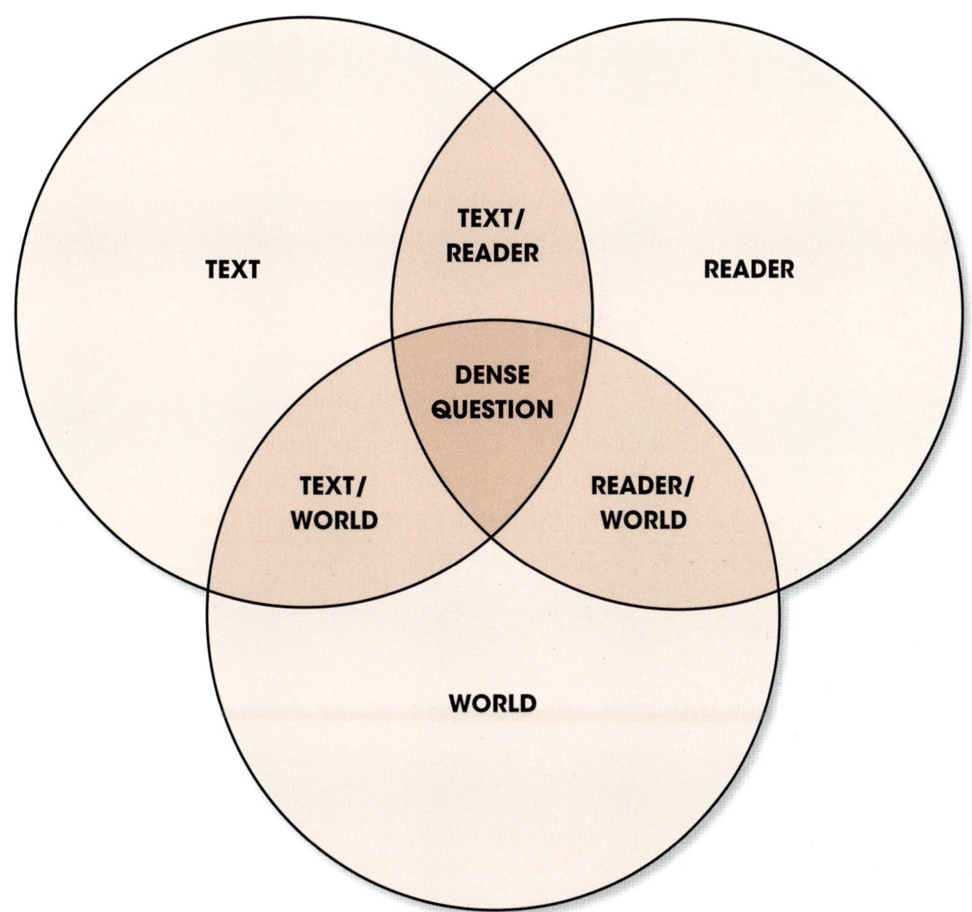

In the unit on freedom vs. security, the collaborative teaching group worked toward reading two extended texts. One text was a graphic novel version of *The Time Machine* by H. G. Wells. This was an excellent choice because the text directly addresses the inquiry question in terms of social class, and the sub-question about the ultimate effects of taking freedom from others. Also, as a visual text, struggling readers were assisted to read and engage in the common project in ways that prepared them to successfully read the second book, *The Giver* by Lois Lowry.

To assist their students to make self-text, text-text, intratextual, and text-world connections with *The Time Machine*, the teachers first used the technique of the questioning circle. This questioning structure requires students to ask and answer questions that are solely from the text, from their personally lived experience, and from what they know about the world and how the inquiry issues play out there. Then students are asked to combine these three resources (personal experience, world knowledge, what is learned from the text) to ask and answer questions that require self-text, text-world, and world-self connections. These questions are known as shaded or combined questions. All of these questions should prepare students to ask and answer what is known as a dense question that requires all three resources to answer and thus requires seeing how the text addresses issues of personal and world importance. This dense question is always a sort of inquiry question.

The teachers provided different models of how to use the scheme over the first sections of the reading, then gradually released responsibility to students to create their own question schemes and answer them, ultimately having small groups create one for the whole book that would be given to another group as the final "test" on the reading. (For fuller treatments supporting questioning circles and explanations of how to use them, see Kelly and Christenbury, 1983; Wilhelm, et al, 2001; Wilhelm, 2007.)

Although teachers may frame the questions, a more powerful strategy is to encourage students to work collaboratively to devise questions using the framework. Introduce students to the idea that the question type is revealed by what resources are used to get the answer, i.e., in thinking carefully about framing a question, the answer to the question is explored and the information necessary to answering it is explored as well.

Example: Questioning Circle

Refer to H. G. Wells' *The Time Machine* (Graphic Novel) and answer the following questions. Be sure to explain your answers when necessary.

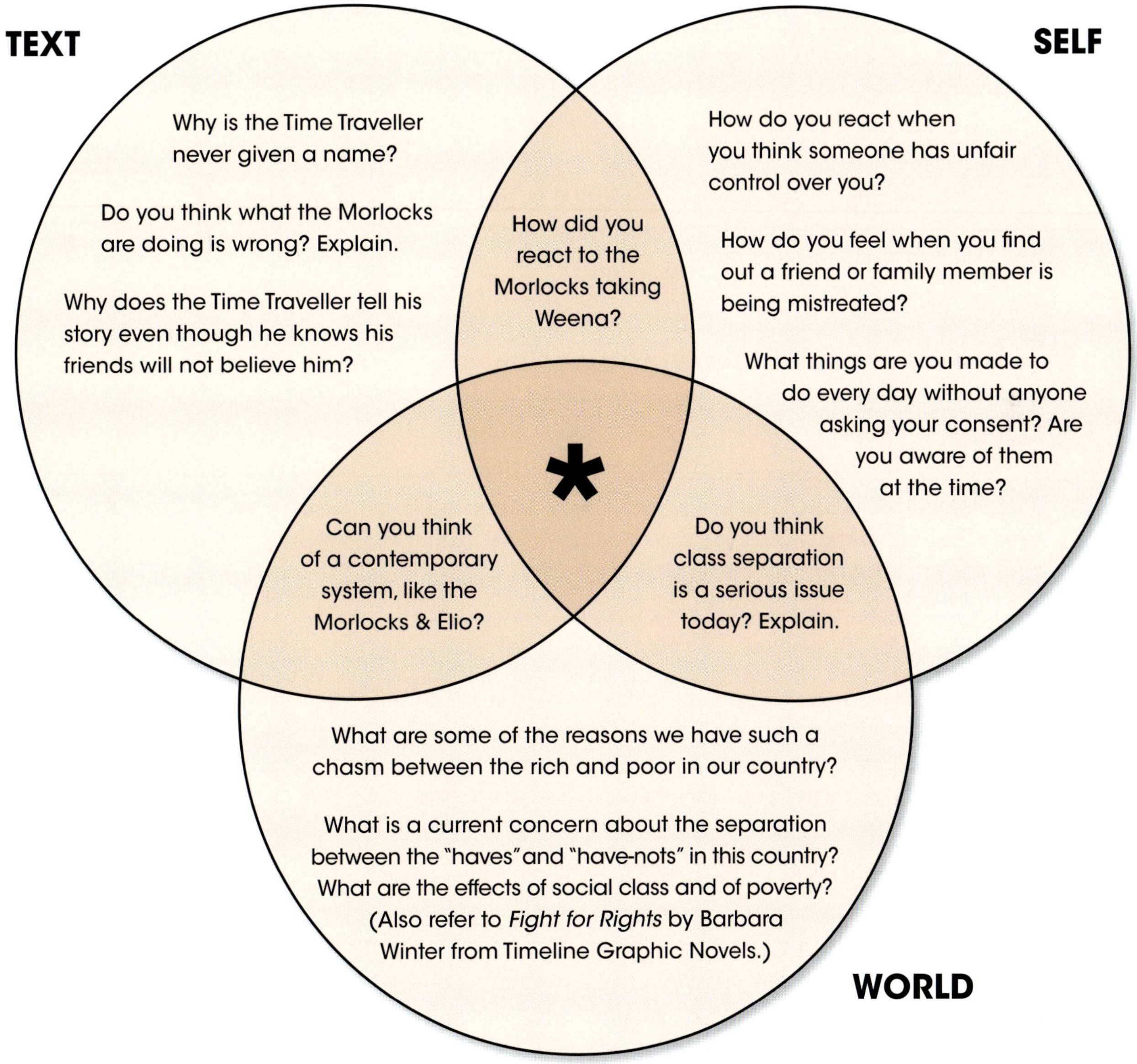

TEXT

Why is the Time Traveller never given a name?

Do you think what the Morlocks are doing is wrong? Explain.

Why does the Time Traveller tell his story even though he knows his friends will not believe him?

TEXT & SELF

How did you react to the Morlocks taking Weena?

SELF

How do you react when you think someone has unfair control over you?

How do you feel when you find out a friend or family member is being mistreated?

What things are you made to do every day without anyone asking your consent? Are you aware of them at the time?

TEXT & WORLD

Can you think of a contemporary system, like the Morlocks & Elio?

SELF & WORLD

Do you think class separation is a serious issue today? Explain.

WORLD

What are some of the reasons we have such a chasm between the rich and poor in our country?

What is a current concern about the separation between the "haves" and "have-nots" in this country? What are the effects of social class and of poverty? (Also refer to *Fight for Rights* by Barbara Winter from Timeline Graphic Novels.)

*

Dense Question (combining self, text, and world resources)

In the story, the Eloi give up the ultimate freedom to be secure (food, clothing). People all over the world give up freedoms for security's sake; list some and analyze them. What do you think are the immediate and ultimate pros and cons of giving up those freedoms?

Guided Reading/Cued Think Aloud

In guided reading, teachers model the kinds of connections they want students to make (or any other strategy they want students to use) by reading and thinking aloud. They then set up situations in which students are mentored or guided to use the strategy. Eventually, students are asked to independently use the strategy through a think aloud (see Wilhelm, 2001) as the teacher monitors their use of this strategy.

This guided reading assignment is designed to aid students in making self-to-text, text-to-text, and text-to-world connections, particularly in regards to the inquiry: Causes and Effects of Migration.

Example: Causes and Effects of Migration

Directions:

1. Read the article on your own. As you read, focus on making self-to-text, text-to-text, and text-to-world connections. Code your connections on the article using s-t, t-t, t-w. You can do this with sticky notes and paste them on the text, or you can use the following template.
2. Once you have read the article on your own, gather with your group and list the self-to-text, text-to-text, text-to-world connections from the group.
3. (Extension) Jigsaw: Form a group of five people who have read five different articles. Using a worksheet (see page 76), list: (1) points of comparison and contrast across all the articles, (2) points of comparison and contrast generated from the cumulative articles and our reading of *The Grapes of Wrath*, and (3) list all the causes and effects of migration that have come up in these readings.

Making Connections:

Self-to-text: Connect your own life experiences with issues discussed in your article. Find profound statements, gems, ideas that speak to all of us. When you read a line, you automatically think about the Joad family, or about the theme of migration. If you have an "ah-ha" moment, write it down.

Text-to-text: Make text-to-text connections between author's viewpoint in your article and the viewpoint of Steinbeck through the way he portrays the Joad family.

Text-to-world: Make text-to-world connections between your article and what you have learned about migrant farm workers in the 1930s, migrant farm workers today, what you hear in the news, and migratory people in general. Also refer to *Boxcar Riders* by Ying S. Lee from Timeline Graphic Novels.

Read the two paragraphs on page 75. They are extracted from "Homeplace" by Scott Russell Sanders. They serve as a think aloud model of how to make connections using s-t, t-t, t-w connections. Teacher comments are in parentheses.

… The Millers dramatize a choice we are faced with constantly: whether to go or stay, whether to move to a situation that is safer, richer, easier, more attractive, or to stick where we are and make what we can of it. ***(t-t:** I wonder if the Joads wished they had stayed in Oklahoma?)* If the shine goes off our marriage, our house, our car, do we trade it for a new one? ***(s-t:** This makes me think about the importance of commitment in my life and what I hope for in a marriage someday.)* If the fertility leaches out of our soil, the creativity out of our job, the money out of our pocket, do we start over somewhere else? ***(s-t:** No, golly, I move so much. I don't mean to, opportunities seem to appear in different places. I long to just settle into one place though. The grass is always greener. I suppose there might be a reason to make changes again, but I think we have to be willing to make sure all possibilities are tapped out first.)* There are voices enough, both inner and outer, urging us to deal with difficulties by pulling up stakes and heading for new territory. I know them well, for they have been calling to me all my days. I wish to raise here a contrary voice, to say a few words on behalf of staying put, learning the ground, going deeper …

The Dust Bowl of the 1930s was caused not by drought but by the transfer onto the Great Plains of farming methods that were suitable to wetter regions. ***(t-t:** Whoa, is this what happened in Oklahoma, to the Joad family?)* The habit of our industry and commerce has been to force identical schemes onto differing locales, as though the mind were a cookie cutter and the land were dough. *(The tractor, brought over from an environment that generally had more rainfall, somehow this tractor dried out the soil on the Great Plains by plowing and leaving soil open to wind and sky. Better to use mounds or seed injectors. (**t-w:** Wow, isn't the same thing happening today? People from elsewhere trying to impose policies or new practices about something they know nothing about. Like milk bottles taken to Africa even though they don't have the capacity to sterilize milk bottles.)*

Now proceed to do the same thing for the article your group has chosen to read. (For a selection of articles on immigration, see *Roots: Uncertain Journeys, New Beginnings* by Rose Fine-Meyer, Harcourt Canada.) Write how you feel the author of your particular article would address these questions and to what degree you would agree or disagree with your author.

» Is it preferable to harmonize or conquer a new situation, to learn new ways of doing things or impose the ways you are used to?

» How does technology affect how we harmonize or impose ways of living on new situations and settings?

» How does the relationship that the average person has with the land affect the environment?

PERSONAL FINDING	ADDITIONAL FINDINGS FROM MY GROUP
Text-to-text:	
Text-to-self:	
Text-to-world:	
Text to our inquiry:	
Points of comparison and contrast across the articles:	
Points of comparison and contrast from cumulative articles:	
What I've learned about the causes and effects of migration:	

NOTE: The techniques of guided reading can be adapted to promote any kind of reading strategy with any topic or text, and deeper conceptual understanding of any kind of inquiry theme.

Free-Response Think Aloud

A useful reading strategy is to have students complete a "Free-Response Think Aloud" to assess their awareness of reading processes. See examples of questions in the table below.

Free-Response Think Aloud	
What are you thinking as you read?	What are you feeling as you read?
What are you doing as you read?	What are you asking as you read?
What are you seeing as you read?	What are you noticing as you read?

The students can be guided into focusing on particular reading strategies as the teacher models a think aloud process. The think aloud process can be used to focus on a specific strategy or to a number of strategies used by expert readers. This is a useful strategy to employ across the different discipline areas as students will encounter a variety of texts to read as they become active participants in inquiry-based learning.

Steps For A Think Aloud

1. Choose a short text (or section of text).
2. Choose one or two strategies to highlight such as asking Q&A questions.
3. State your purpose(s) and how the strategies will work to serve the purpose.
4. Read the text aloud to students and think aloud, highlighting how you use the strategies as you do so.
5. Underline the words and phrases that helped you notice that the strategy would be useful or that helped you to use it.
6. List (name) the strategies used.
7. Identify other situations (real-world reading situations) in which students could use these strategies.
8. Reinforce with follow-up lessons.

(For full descriptions of various ways to use think alouds to teach various strategies and genre conventions, see Wilhelm, 2001)

STRATEGY 13 Anticipation/Reaction Guide

Another useful strategy to guide students in their reading is the Anticipation/Reaction Guide. This strategy promotes active reading, discussion, and critical thinking. This pre-reading strategy helps the reader activate prior knowledge and determine the purpose for reading. The strategy also serves as a focus for reading by identifying important points or major concepts. The teacher can use this strategy to identify prior knowledge as well as highlight misconceptions. The aim is for the reader to make predictions about the reading and then be encouraged to search for evidence which supports each of the prediction statements.

Anticipation/Prediction Reading Guide

- Identify the major concepts to be learned in the text or appropriate information source being used.
- Create 3 to 10 statements that support or challenge the student's beliefs and experiences about the topic.
- Statements may focus on important points, major concepts, controversial ideas, or misconceptions.
- Arrange statements in the order in which the concepts are dealt within the text.
- Students agree or disagree.
- Students discuss in pairs or small groups.
- Reread the selection with the purpose of finding evidence to determine the validity of the positions they took during the pre-reading step, or to change those positions.
- During the post-reading step, students are asked to confirm their original predications, revise them, discard them, or decide what additional information is needed.

Notice that this activity activates and builds on what students already know (since other students will know and think things they do) before they read *and* focuses attention on and organizes what is learned *during* reading. It also provides a placeholding device for reflecting on what has been learned *after* reading.

Example: Spiders

Spiders are the only arachnid with special glands in their belly to make silk and weave webs. Once their web is woven, spiders sit and wait for their next meal to be trapped in it. But not all spiders live in webs. Some live in burrows and hunt on the ground. They either wait for their prey to wander by or go out and hunt for food. Although spiders do prefer to sink their teeth into other bugs, most will bite human beings if they feel trapped. ...

Most hunting spiders inject their meals with paralyzing venom and then dig in. Web builders don't always like to chomp down right away. They usually wrap their victim with the same silk used to build their web — kind of like wrapping a fajita! The black widow and brown recluse spiders are two of the world's most deadly. A painful black widow bite makes your muscles go stiff and stops you from breathing. The bite of a brown recluse is just as bad, causing your flesh to rot and die.

(From *The 10 Grossest Bugs*)

Black widow spiders are the largest web weavers.

After reading the text, students complete the assignment below.	BEFORE READING	AFTER READING
All spiders are poisonous.	☐	☐
Spiders eat mostly plants.	☐	☐
The black widow spider is dangerous.	☐	☐
You should stay away from the brown recluse spider.	☐	☐
Spiders may be creepy, but they are useful.	☐	☐

How has your thinking on the topic changed?

____

Cite information that supports your choices.

YES	HOW IS MY CHOICE SUPPORTED?	NO	WHY IS MY CHOICE NOT CORRECT?
☐	________________	☐	________________
☐	________________	☐	________________
☐	________________	☐	________________
☐	________________	☐	________________
☐	________________	☐	________________

Reciprocal Reading

Reciprocal Teaching (Palincsar and Brown, 1984) is a technique with a powerful supporting research base. It demonstrates that it assists and helps students to use general processes of reading. We have adapted the technique to also focus on task- and text-specific strategies of reading and call our version of it Reciprocal Reading. In this example, you will see how the technique can be used with short segments of text to promote both general processes like summarizing, and more task-specific strategies like asking questions that require making connections or making particular kinds of connections. These processes both support and enhance inquiry-based learning.

Reciprocal Reading Assignment

Work in groups of four. There are four jobs for the group, and everyone will get a chance at every job. Decide who will be reading first. The four jobs are Reader/Predictor, Questioner, Summarizer, and Connector. Starting with the Reader/Predictor, the jobs are assigned in a counter-clockwise direction. On a blank sheet of paper, write the name of your job across the top.

Reader/Predictor:

Your job is to read the section of text aloud. After everyone else has done their jobs, the group will come back to you and you will make a prediction about what will happen based on what you read. Your prediction can be for something that will happen right away or later in the story, and it doesn't matter if you're right or wrong here. Share the prediction with the group and discuss its merit based on the text. Once the group decides your prediction is plausible, write the prediction and your reasons for the prediction on your sheet.

Questioner:

Your job is to come up with a QAR (Raphael, 1986) think and search question (requiring an intratextual connection or connections to answer) based on the section of text that was just read. Share the question with the group and discuss how you know your question requires thinking and searching across the text and connecting various pieces of different information from this and previous chapters together. Then discuss possible answers until the group can come up with an answer that satisfies everyone. Once all group members agree on the answer, write both the question and answer on your sheet. (An additional or adapted role could be to ask a QAR Author and Me question requiring a self-text connection to be made, or a Questioning Circle self-text, or text-world question.)

Summarizer:

Your job is to summarize the passage of text that was just read. Share your summary with the group and discuss whether or not it is complete. Encourage other group members to add to it if you left something out, or delete anything that is not absolutely essential. Once the whole group is happy with the summary, write it on your sheet.

Connector:

Your job is to make a connection between what you have just read and something outside the reading of this particular segment. This could be a connection to something in your life (self-text), a connection to something earlier in the text (intratextual connection), or something from another text, particularly one we have read previously in this unit (text-to-text) though you could also connect it to other movies, articles, or cartoons with which you are familiar. Explain the connection to the group and discuss whether the connection makes sense based on what was read. When all group members understand the connection and agree it makes sense, write the connection on your sheet. (This could be adapted to focus on a different kind of connection, such as connecting something in this chapter to the inquiry theme, or to the world.)

These are all things that expert readers do as they read. Whenever you read something, you should be doing all of these in your head in order to better understand it. This is something that will happen automatically as you become better readers, but this exercise gives you some practice to consciously think about and use each strategy in a group.

The trick is that after completing your work with each passage of text (sections identified by the teacher), you will pass your sheet and job to the right. This way, everyone gets a chance to do each job, with the help of your classmates, of course! When you are finished, staple the group sheets together and make sure all four names are on the first page. The grading will be based on the collective group responses, so make sure that each group member does a good job.

To continue this idea, use this technique individually for the rest of the book. After every few pages, stop and ask a think-and-search question, summarize what's going on, make a connection of some sort, and predict what will happen next. This will be your reading response for the rest of the book, so keep a log to be turned in.

Reciprocal Reading Cards

Reader/Predictor:

The predictor offers guesses about what the author will tell next or what the next events in the story will be.

Questioner:

The questioner poses questions about the selection:

» Unclear parts
» Puzzling information
» Connections to other concepts
» Motivations of author or characters

Summarizer:

The summarizer highlights the key ideas in the reading.

Connector:

The connector makes a connection between what is read and something outside the reading of this particular segment.

Literature Circles

For teachers who use literature circles, specific roles can be designed to encourage specific kinds of reading activity (e.g., symbol seeker, connection maker, text-inquiry connector, etc.).

Establishing effective literature circles requires planning, training, reflecting, and plenty of time. Harvey Daniels (2002) provides the following steps:

» Provide a wide choice of texts. Ask students to get into groups of four or five.
» Review use of response logs.
» Give a set amount of time for reading and some writing (dependent on age level). Have groups assign themselves a section for reading to be finished in five minutes less than the allotted time. The last five minutes is used for recording their responses on their different sheets.
» After reading, members come together to have a "natural conversation" about the text, sharing what they recorded in their role sheets.
» Observe the groups and note specific behaviours and examples that either hinder or help the process.
» As a class, debrief the process. What behaviours were helpful (eye contact, nodding in agreement) and what hindered the process (interrupting, getting off topic)? Make a list and review the examples before the next set of circles.
» Assign groups to read sections for the next meeting. Remind them to use the response logs.

When completing an inquiry unit, students can be introduced to a variety of texts related to the topic of inquiry. They can then select which text their group chooses to read and how they will proceed to complete the reading. This process can be used for both works of literature and short pieces of text. On completion, the groups can select a way to make a presentation to the class. For a further discussion on literature circles, refer to *Literature Circles: Voice and Choice in Book Clubs and Reading Groups* by Harvey Daniels.

When designing reading and think aloud activities, think about ...

» How do you encourage connection-making through your reading activities?
» What opportunities do you provide for students' personal meaning making and student choice?
» How do you explicitly teach or model each reading strategy?

STRATEGIES FOR GROUPING

A variety of groupings within the classroom is important to promote student discussion, meaning making, procedural and conceptual knowledge exploration, reading discussions, and connection of ideas. Different group structures allow students to participate in a democratic classroom, and participate in different roles within a group as well as be efficient in the social learning setting.

Knowing the purpose of the grouping helps teachers to establish effective communities. Teachers should think about the purpose of the task, the students' likes and dislikes, readiness, as well as the leadership qualities to be developed by each member. Regular assigned groups such as literature circles, writing groups, etc. should be changed on a regular basis. Through an inquiry approach, we often switch groups within a class period setting.

Moving quickly from group to group is sometimes a concern for teachers new to inquiry. However, we've found established routines, cues, and assigned meeting places allow students to move quickly from group to group. Most teachers find their own processes that work well.

Random assigning can also be done occasionally and ways to group quickly include:

- Person next to you
- Coloured popsicle sticks handed out at the door
- Matching buttons or blocks — given out at the door
- Number off
- Out of the hat
- Puzzle pieces to form your group — each person gets a puzzle piece
- Question and answer to jokes
- Choosing one partner and then pairing up with another partner by the teacher (allows for some student choice)
- Balancing the boat (see Tool Kit section)

You will see how randomly assigning groupings also involves community building among the students.

Jigsaw Reading

Jigsaw reading is useful for grouping students for discussion as well as a useful reading strategy. The students are assigned home groups or base groups. The key idea is that the individual members of the home group are responsible and accountable for sharing the level of knowledge and understanding that the home group will develop. Each individual member of the home group then numbers off and forms an expert group with other members of the class that share the same number so that they bring different areas of expertise to a new group. This process is listed below:

1. Students form home groups of 4 or 5 students each.
2. Students in the home group number off: 1, 2, 3, 4, (5).
3. All 1's form an expert group. So do all 2's, 3's, etc.
4. Each expert group is given a topic, section of text, part of a problem or task to complete. Each expert group must fully understand their assignment and be able to teach it to their home group. Expert groups plan how to teach their material to their home groups.
5. All students return to their home group — each will share what they learned in the expert group.

One way of teaching is for the expert group to display their information on paper. Participants then return to their home groups and teach all members of their group as they are now the experts. As a co-operative group, they can be asked to fill in a placemat of their new knowledge (see Strategy 17).

Another way is for participants to return to their home groups and then take their co-operative group on a Gallery Tour. They walk around the room to view the displays that other groups have created. In this way, a larger text or task is divided up — or jig-sawed among different students.

Gallery Walk

The gallery walk is a useful way to have students share their ideas and work, get responses to these, see patterns across other students' work and responses, and provide the stimulation for both formal and informal discussions.

Individual or small groups of students first create a visible response to a question or problem, or even ask a question of their own. The response can be in visual form, such as a picture map that tells the journey of their thinking, a thinking chart, a Venn diagram, etc., or it can be simply written on chart paper.

Next, get students to post their work. Have students count off by 1's and 2's, then give half of the students in the classroom time to walk around the "gallery of work" and listen as the "presenters" who stayed at home with their work talk about what they have done. An informal discussion can then ensue between presenter and visitor, or as a larger group, once everyone has seen all the work presentations.

Keep the time short, asking students to visit four or five exhibits in a 6-8 minute time block. Then ask the gallery walkers to return to their work, and allow those who were presenting to tour the gallery of exhibits.

Those visiting can write responses on sticky notes, and then post these on or near the exhibit they are commenting on. These can be helpful comments about what to do next, ideas to add or consider, questions, or just general responses about things they noticed or learned from the exhibit and its presentation. Post-it notes can be initialled, so that presenters can take the Post-its and follow up with the questioner.

As a group, students can begin to look for commonalities, differences, themes, new questions to pursue, etc., across the exhibits that can then be categorized, e.g., "What do they notice, wonder, or question" when perusing the gallery of ideas? The collated notes and feedback from this activity can then form the basis for a whole class discussion.

When using a placemat graphic organizer, each student has the opportunity to track the thinking and discussion in each group or at different stations on a gallery walk. Then upon returning to their original groups, students can relay information and create a summary in the centre of the placemat. All of the processes are important in synthesizing and organizing information.

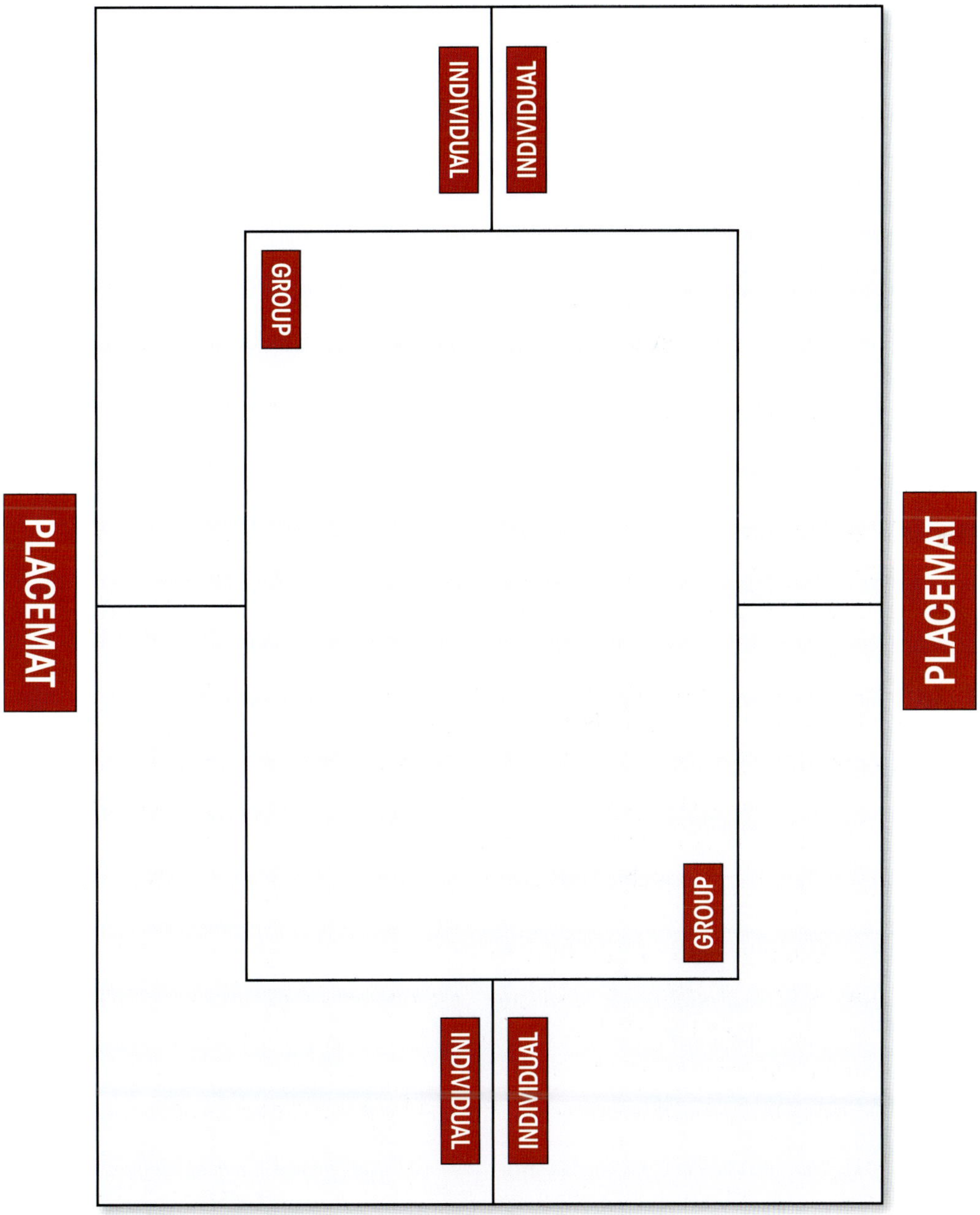

INDIVIDUAL
INDIVIDUAL
GROUP
PLACEMAT
PLACEMAT
GROUP
INDIVIDUAL
INDIVIDUAL

Carousel Seating

This strategy is a useful one to engage students in a discussion about the inquiry topic and/or assigned reading. Students sit in two concentric circles. The "inner circle" turn out to face the outer circle — who face in. When time is called, the outer circle move around one position and each student has a new discussion partner to share ideas and elaborate with.

It is useful to have a prompt or question for students to discuss. An example would be: "What dangers could people face through using the Internet?" This discussion could also double as a classroom community-building exercise on establishing norms for computer use in the classroom.

le Edit View History Bookmarks Window Tools Help

SYSTEM FAILURE

Without a doubt, the Internet is one of the greatest inventions of all time. Where else can you see artwork from museums in countries around the world, find information on just about anything, and chat with your friends — all simply by typing a few words on your keyboard? But despite all of these benefits, the Internet also has its share of problems.

The Internet can be a place where sneaky criminals hide out. They use their superb computer skills to steal money or to crack computer codes to cause major damage! Problems with the Internet can cause emotional or physical pain — pain that can take years to heal.

In choosing and ranking the 10 worst things about the Internet, we considered the following: the damage caused, the number of people affected, whether the damage can be fixed, and whether it can be stopped.

So before you log on and get caught in the Web, try to decide:

WHAT IS THE WORST THING ABOUT THE INTERNET?

(From *The 10 Worst Things About the Internet*)

Inside/Outside Circles

In this strategy, the inside circle (seated) hold a discussion and the outside circle (standing) observe. Each outside circle member evaluates the participation of the student directly in front and those sitting on either side (an idea is to use an evaluation sheet — see below). This is a useful strategy to pair and group students for discussion purposes. Places are then flipped as the inside circle become the outside circle. Students on the outside can record what students on the inside do, particularly strategies or "moves" that the teacher might be encouraging.

Sample Evaluation Form: Student Discussion

Student names	Added new insight	Specific reference to the text being discussed	Attentive listening behaviours	Appreciation of others

STRATEGY 21

Silent Discussion Thread

Organize the class into groups and provide each student with a piece of paper with a question written on the top of the sheet (about five questions for the class, each group will have the same five questions). After "time" is called, each student passes the paper to his/her left and the next student responds (see response guidelines below). No one should talk! After everyone in the group has responded, a small group or whole class discussion can ensue.

Silent Discussion Guidelines:

- Each member in your group will receive a sheet with one question at the top. (This could be from your teacher or from another student.) Each of you will have a different question.
- Compose a response to the question. Your teacher may time you to encourage you to finish your response in one to two minutes.
- When "time" is called, pass your sheet to the person on your left; receive a new sheet from the person on your right.
- Read the question and response(s) on the new sheet.
- Add something new to the response to the question. You may build on, expand, extend, or disagree with prior responses.
- Pass the sheet to your left; receive a new sheet. Repeat until everyone in the group has had a chance to respond to each question.

A good resource to use for the silent discussion thread is *The 10 Most Influential Speeches in World History* (Scholastic Canada). Allow students to read extracts from this book to answer the question "What makes a speech powerful?" In order to answer this big question, the students can take turns to respond to sub-questions such as "What language devices were used?" "What was the purpose of the speech?" "How did the speech influence the audience?" After the silent discussion, a verbal discussion could be pursued, based on what the group has written.

Note that it is a good idea to have each person in the group initial their responses and that there is an expectation for the small groups to have a member report back their responses from the group.

Round Robins and Anchor Charts

Round Robins is a grouping technique that helps students to quickly brainstorm. The teacher provides several anchor charts with different headings that designate topics or ideas related to the inquiry problem or task at hand. Each group of students has two minutes to put as much information as possible on the chart. When the bell rings, each group moves and adds new material to the new chart. This could work as frontloading, but also as a reflection and discussion technique on what has just been read or learned.

Anchor charts make classroom knowledge visible. Students can track brainstorming, complete K-W-H-L charts, placehold important information as well as follow throughlines and threads of thinking.

When designing groups for collaboration or discussion, think about...

- Start with small groups before moving to large-group discussions.
- Set a clear task and accountability procedure — something to be produced and shared.
- Set a time limit for small group tasks. For longer projects, have the students "check in" on their progress. Shorter time frames are better than longer ones.
- Be ever present. When students work in groups, the teacher must be very active, monitoring and assisting, but only intervening when it is necessary.
- Have small groups report and share what they have done.
- Provide some closure, reflection, and consolidation of what has been discussed and learned.
- An idea is to ask groups to set a new "moving forward" task, such as identifying something to find out about or discuss later.

Boxing

Students can create meaning through writing questions and answers with partners or small groups in order to explore topics. Here the students can write questions inside a box and then pass to another group who answer and/or ask new questions in the next outer layer of the box. Students initial their responses and questions. This can help teachers to track the students' thinking.

Below is an example of boxing, framed around the question: "What do you believe is happening in the world today that requires the government to create laws to protect us?"

What do you believe is happening in the world today that requires the government to create laws to protect us?

SWOT Analysis

This template allows students to divide into groups to discuss the strengths, weaknesses, opportunities, and threats regarding a particular issue, proposal, situation, character, or of an explanation revealed in a particular reading. Students can add sticky notes with their ideas to a giant chart and then discuss in pairs or small groups their own ideas and the relationship of these ideas to those of others. Or they can use the template below in a group, which will require discussion.

The template is a SWOT analysis that students completed to reflect upon a social action project designed to support participants in the Special Olympics. (Some teachers prefer to use "obstacles," "risks," or "hazards" instead of "threats," depending on the topic and situation.)

Strengths	Weaknesses
» We had a great idea and our group all participated. » We made contacts in the community. » We were committed to making it happen. » We worked hard to get sponsorship.	» We rushed to meet deadlines and it got crazy there for a while. » We didn't advertise until the end. » We had to throw the first batch of cookies away.
Opportunities	**Threats**
» We made great contacts with business. » We could run the "cookie bake" again next year. » We could do more to publicize the event.	» Some of our classmates were not supportive and didn't think we could do it. » We received sponsorship late. » Another group could steal our idea.

STRATEGY 25

Socratic Seminar

Once discussion protocols have been established, moving students on to participate in seminars is the next step in inquiry-based learning. Good seminars occur when participants study the text closely in advance, listen attentively, share their ideas and questions in response to the ideas and questions of others, and search for evidence in the text to support their ideas. Discussion is between students with the teacher guiding and directing when needed. When participants realize that the leader is not looking for right answers but is encouraging them to think out loud and to exchange ideas openly, they discover the excitement of exploring important issues through shared inquiry. This excitement creates willing participants, eager to examine ideas in a rigorous, thoughtful manner.

Students sit in a circle and share conversation. Teachers often find it helpful to track the conversation using a camera.

Guidelines for participants in a Socratic seminar:

- Refer to the text when needed during the discussion. A seminar is not a test of memory. You are not "learning a subject," and your goal is to understand the ideas, issues, and values reflected in the text.
- It's okay to "pass" when asked to contribute.
- Ask for clarification when confused.
- Stick to the point currently under discussion; make notes about ideas you want to come back to.
- Take turns when speaking, raising hands are not needed. Students depend upon nonverbal cues about taking turns to speak.
- Listen carefully.
- Speak up so that all can hear you.
- Talk to each other, not just to the leader or teacher.
- Discuss ideas rather than each other's opinions.
- Every student is responsible for the seminar.

Teachers teach specific reading and thinking strategies that students practise within this seminar. Assessment occurs with what the seminar is emphasizing. With this seminar, teachers can name and/or re-focus students' attention to a variety of different strategies.

A possible assessment might be to ask if the participants:

- » speak loudly and clearly?
- » cite reasons and evidence for their statements?
- » use the text to find support?
- » listen to others respectfully?
- » stick with the subject?
- » talk to one another, not just to the leader?
- » paraphrase accurately?
- » avoid inappropriate language (slang, technical terms, sloppy diction, etc.)?
- » ask for help to clear up confusion?
- » support one another?
- » question others in a civil manner?

Debate	**Dialogue**
Two opposing sides try to prove each other wrong.	Remains open-ended.
One listens to find flaws, to spot differences, and to counter arguments.	One listens to understand, to make meaning, and to find common ground.
One defends assumptions as truth.	Enlarges and possibly changes a participant's point of view.
Creates a closed-minded attitude, a determination to be right.	Creates an open-minded attitude, openness to being wrong and openness to change.
One submits one's best thinking and defends it against challenges to show that it is right.	One submits one's best thinking, expecting that other people's reflections will help improve it rather than threaten it.
Calls for investing wholeheartedly in one's beliefs.	Calls for temporarily suspending one's beliefs.
One searches for weaknesses in the other position.	One searches for strengths in all positions.
Rebuts contrary positions and may belittle or deprecate other participants.	Respects all the other participants and seeks not to alienate or offend.
Assumes a single right answer that somebody already has.	Assumes that many people have pieces of answers and that co-operation can lead to a greater understanding.
Debate demands a conclusion.	Dialogue does not.

Teachers explain the difference between dialogue and debate.

Dialogue is characterized by:

- suspending judgement
- examining our own work without defensiveness
- exposing our reasoning and looking for limits to it
- communicating our underlying assumptions
- exploring viewpoints more broadly and deeply
- being open to disconfirming data
- approaching someone who sees a problem differently not as an adversary, but as a colleague in common pursuit of better solutions
- multiple sides working toward shared understanding

Sample questions that demonstrate constructive participation in discussion circles are:

- Here is my view and how I arrived at it. How does it sound to you?
- What gaps do you see in my reasoning?
- What data do you have that is different?
- How is your conclusion different?
- How did you arrive at your view?
- What are you taking into account that is different from what I have considered?

STRATEGIES FOR QUESTIONING AND CONNECTION MAKING

Throughout an inquiry unit, the essential question is the omnipresent anchor. Everything that is read and learned must connect in some way to addressing and understanding issues related to the question.

Learners generate questions through all inquiry activities: frontloading, guided learning activities, reading, problem-solving and discussions, and so forth. They ask questions to:

» clarify meaning
» predict solutions
» speculate about readings
» deepen their comprehension
» reply to other students' thoughts
» pursue ideas
» be critical
» be reflective
» see patterns

Three-Level Questioning Guide

The three-level questioning strategy was first devised by Herber (1978) and developed further by Morris and Stewart-Dore (1984) to help students think through information in the texts and to move beyond the surface level. This is achieved as the students begin to recognize that in order to fully engage with a text they must 1) grasp the established facts, 2) see patterns and make inferences among the facts, and 3) consider how to creatively transfer and apply what has been learned. This, in fact, is the inquiry process in miniature. Any questioning scheme that mirrors this process (like QARs) promotes inquiry and deepens understanding.

The following is a template that we have used, as well as some questions that students generated when they began to look critically at an advertisement. Firstly, the students asked questions that they could find direct answers to within the text. At level two, they began to ask interpretive questions based on what was seen in the text as well as their own information and knowledge. At level three, they began to generate questions that formed the basis of their own student-led inquiry projects. (See also Strategy 3 on pages 60–61.)

Three-Level Questioning	
Questioning level	**Evidence from the text**
Level 1: On the Lines Also known as literal or "right there" questions. This is the simplest kind of question. The student might be asked to: » identify the main idea of the paragraph, if directly stated » recall simple details » organize the sequence in which the main events occurred Examples of on the line question starters: » What happened ...? » How many ...? » How did ...? » Who ...? » What is ...? » Which ...?	

(Continued)

Level 2: Between the Lines Also known as inferential or "think and search" questions. The reader searches for various clues in the text and adds them together and interprets the pattern to find the answer. The student might be asked to: » anticipate endings and consequences » state reasons for events » make generalizations Examples of between the line question starters: » Why did …? » What was …? » What do you think about …? » Can you explain …? » How was this similar to …?	
Level 3: Beyond the Lines Also known as evaluative, critical, applicative, or "on my own" questions. The readers make links between the text and their own experiences and knowledge to find the answer. The question is open-ended, promotes rich discussion, and deeper understanding. The reader needs to justify the answer. The student might be asked to: » make generalizations » make comparisons » make judgements » make recommendations and suggestions » make decisions » create alternative endings Examples of beyond-the-line question starters: » Do you think that … should have …? » What else could she/you …? » How would you …? » Do you agree …?	

Question-Answer Relationship

Question-Answer Relationship is often referred to as QAR. QAR has a variety of adaptations that can be used to assist readers and learners to delve into the deeper meaning of text and critical topics. Teachers set this up in numerous ways. Charts, T-charts, Venn diagrams, writing responses, and discussion circles can all be used.

QAR question types follow the trajectory of On, Between, and Beyond the Lines. They move from factual questions to interpretive ones to evaluative queries. Raphael (1986) divides questions into four types: Right There questions, Think and Search questions, Author and Me questions, and On My Own questions.

RIGHT THERE:
These questions are factual, requiring students to find the spot in the text where the question is answered. You can literally find the answers "right there" in the text.

THINK AND SEARCH:
These questions are interpretive — they require the reader to identify various spots in a text where information related to the question is stated. The reader must "search" for the various details and "think" about the nature of the connection between the details. If the details are close together, the question is easier to answer and constitutes a "simple implied relationship" question. If there are many details, and they are less obviously related, then the question can be considered a "complex implied relationship."

AUTHOR AND ME:
These questions require the readers to bring their own knowledge to bear on a text. Such questions might require readers to fill in gaps in the text by providing prior knowledge and information from their own lives that would reasonably fit, or to provide an elaboration and extension of the text that is based on their experience. Students must be able to bring knowledge from their personal life, prior reading, or the world in combination with the text to answer this question type.

ON MY OWN:
These questions do not require textual information from the specific reading, though having read the text might have stimulated the question or assisted in some way in addressing it. Inquiry questions are often questions of this type; for instance, you can tentatively answer the question of "What makes a speech powerful?" or "What makes a good relationship?" without having completed a particular reading, although readings might help you answer it. These questions are evaluative or applicative: answers that typically stake a claim about the world or potential actions that could be taken.

MAKE POVERTY HISTORY

"Millions of people in the world's poorest countries remain imprisoned, enslaved, and in chains. They are trapped in the prison of poverty."

These powerful words came from an 87-year-old who had just retired. Nelson Mandela, former president of South Africa, told the crowds at the London rally against poverty that he really shouldn't be there. He had recently retired from public life. "However, as long as poverty, injustice, and gross inequality persist in our world, none of us can truly rest."

He was asked to speak by the Campaign to Make Poverty History. Its goal is to improve the life of the poorest nations. Mandela knew how destructive poverty could be. In his home country of South Africa, life had been a prison for millions who couldn't afford life's basic necessities.

"Like slavery and apartheid, poverty is not natural," Mandela said. "It is man-made and it can be overcome and eradicated by the actions of human beings." To Mandela, having a decent life was a basic human right. Rich nations could help with fair trade, debt relief for poor countries, and more aid to them.

(From *The 10 Most Influential Speeches in World History*, page 27)

RIGHT THERE:
Why did Mandela tell the crowds that he really shouldn't be there?

THINK AND SEARCH:
Why was Mandela asked to give a speech by the Campaign to Make Poverty History?

AUTHOR AND ME:
If you were Nelson Mandela, what might you have said in the speech?

ON MY OWN:
If your country were ever taken over by an authority you disagreed with, what would you do? What would you be uncompromising about?

QARs in Science

QAR works very well to promote expertise in reading because good readers and inquirers must address all question types to truly and deeply understand. Likewise, QARs replicate what content area experts do to understand a text or a data set. For example, in a brainstorming session, science teachers from our national demo site discussed how the QAR scheme can engage students in the kinds of thinking and inquiry valued in science (Wilhelm, 2007):

RIGHT THERE:
Promote careful observation and consider direct evidence.

THINK AND SEARCH:
Promote seeing relationships among data and the seeing of patterns across data sets. Promote the making of reasonable inferences and hypotheses, and a consideration of indirect evidence to make predictions, and to theorize. Encourages students to study data to see patterns and to make reasonable inferences based on data patterns.

AUTHOR AND ME:
Promote creating mental models and extending these for use in altered contexts. Promote personal innovation and engagement with scientific ideas and processes as it leads to experimentation, intervention, and the creation of new data to add to what is already established, or to confirm or disconfirm hypotheses. Encourage critical inquiry and the active agency of students to become practitioners as they converse with existing data and add to existing data sets.

ON MY OWN:
Promote the application of scientific concepts and processes, making connections between scientific learning and real-world issues and problems. Promote testing generalizations and being a scientific thinker in the world.

The Expert Says ...

> "The invention of the telescope ... marked the birth of the modern scientific method and set the stage for a dramatic reassessment of our place in the cosmos."
>
> — Brian Greene, professor of physics and mathematics, Columbia University

(From *The 10 Most Revolutionary Inventions*)

QARs in Math

RIGHT THERE:
Establish the facts and understand the details from the data/text. Identify unnecessary information/distractors.

THINK AND SEARCH:
Discern patterns and relationships in the data; infer proper operations necessary to solve the problem.

AUTHOR AND ME:
Consider how to find missing information that might be helpful. Identify a meaningful context in which solving this kind of problem would be useful in your life. Identify and apply proper operations. Consider alternative operations and ways of solving the problem, as well as the costs and benefits, and efficiencies and inefficiencies of each. Check work. Evaluate effectiveness of your procedures. Hypothesize and articulate general principles. Test hypotheses. Decision and meaning making by the student is foregrounded.

ON MY OWN:
Consider real-world applications of general principles and problem-solving procedures. Identify situations in which concepts and strategies can be used. Think like a mathematician as you go through your daily life.

STRATEGY 28

Question Prompts

To encourage topical research and extend it to critical inquiry, it is useful for the teacher to use question prompts. We have found that this is most successful when continually used throughout the unit or learning sequence in the form of before, during, and after questions. Using prompts encourages students to elaborate and extend their thinking.

Before Reading

To help students activate prior knowledge, ask …

- What do you already know about this topic/idea/problem/issue?
- What does the topic/term/concept/phrase/statement (regarding the essential question) remind you of or mean to you?

Share an artifact, photograph, film clip, formula, etc. regarding the topic or essential question and ask …

- What do you think this artifact means?
- Why is it significant?
- What will it have to do with our inquiry? Why might learning about this be important?
- Describe some ways in which this problem/topic comes up in everyday living.

During and After Reading

To make interpretive connections among ideas and applications, ask …

- How does this relate to X?
- What ideas that we have learned before were useful in solving this problem/reading this text/understanding this situation?
- How is this similar to another event/concept/problem/process/story you already knew about?
- Can you give me an example?
- What relationship does/might … have to our class/school/ life/community?
- What uses of mathematics/science/history/language did you find in the newspaper this morning? On the news? At your home?
- How does X relate to Y?
- Give examples of how X comes up in other situations outside this content area?

To help students reason across data patterns, ask …

» Is that true for all cases? Explain.
» In how many ways is X similar to Y?
» In how many ways are X and Y different?
» What is the criterion or rule that would run across cases?
» Can you think of a counter example?
» How would you prove it?
» What assumptions are you making?
» How can you test your assumptions? How can you revise your assumptions in the face of disconfirming data?
» In what ways can you tell the difference between X and Y? The similarities?
» Provide ways you could tell that this example belongs to this category or type? Does not belong?

To encourage conjecturing and interpretation, ask …

» What would happen if …? What would happen if not?
» Under what conditions would this explanation/strategy/principle not work?
» Do you see a pattern? Can you explain the pattern?
» Extrapolate the pattern. Can you predict the next example in the pattern?
» Interpolate the pattern. Predict a missing element or an element between the existing elements in the pattern.
» Elaborate on the pattern.
» What are some other possibilities we might find in the patterns?
» What insights can be reached/decisions can be made based on the data?
» What use should/could the understandings be put to?

To promote topical research / critical inquiry and problem-solving, ask …

» What do you need to find out?
» What information do you have?
» What information do you still need? How can you get it? How can you produce new data?
» What strategies will you need to use?
» What tools will you need?
» What resources are available or could be developed?
» What do you think the answer or result will be? Why do you think this? Why might it be different than we expect?

To help students converse with an author (or another student / thinker) and make collective sense of a text, ask …

- What does the author want us to know/believe/do?
- Do you understand what … is saying? What would help you understand it more fully?
- What do you think about what … said/wrote/argued?
- Do you agree? Why or why not?
- Does anyone take the same position/have the same answer but a different way to explain it/justify/reach it?
- How can you convince the rest of us that your answer/process/idea makes sense?

After Reading

To encourage understanding from multiple perspectives, evaluation, and reflection, ask …

- What did you find most interesting, or confusing, or difficult?
- What more do you want/need to know about the topic?
- How did you address the problem/get your answer?
- What might be another way of solving the problem? Looking at the problem?
- Does your solution seem reasonable and useful? Why or why not?
- Describe your problem-solving method to the rest of us, and why you used it, found it effective, etc.
- What if you started with … rather than …?
- I wonder what would happen if …
- What if this or that condition changed?
- How could you use these ideas or processes to solve a current problem/ in the future?
- Describe an obstacle or pitfall to avoid and how to avoid it when pursuing a similar task.
- When you do this again, what will your remember? What will you do differently?
- Explain your process/essential steps for completing this task.
- What should the teacher do differently next year to improve learning?

To consolidate understanding, ask …

- What have you learned or found out today?
- What were the most important points/strategies to remember from today?
- How was X important? How will you use it?

» What are the key points/big understandings of the lesson?
» Summarize what you have learned in words your reading buddy from a younger grade would understand.
» Why are these things important?
» If these things are true, what might follow? How might we use this understanding in other problems?
» Describe how you know you understand/can do something better as a result of the lesson or unit.
» How can we name our changes in understanding?
» What kind of metaphors could explain our understanding?

Example: Before, During, After Questioning

Students were introduced to an extract of the *Lord of the Flies* as a thought provoking prompt into democratic decision making as part of a unit on 'What makes a democracy?' The student-generated "before" questions helped to tune in their thinking, the "during" allowed them to participate with the text and the "after," to go beyond the text and more broadly into the inquiry unit on democracy.

Before

» What will this reading have to do with rules?
» What does Lord refer to? Flies? (Is Lord like a leader? Who might be flies?)
» How might this story be tied to ideas about democracy?

During

» Why did the boys choose Ralph to be a leader?
» Why is it important that Ralph keeps Jack 'on side'?
» Why do the boys decide to vote?

After

» What qualities does a good leader have?
» How should voters decide among candidates?
» When faced with an emergency, is being strong all that matters?
» What should a society do when facing an emergency?
» What might happen after the emergency is over?
» Does a leader making decisions alone make the best decisions?
» Is fast action more important than a lot of talking and checking?

(From New Norfolk High School Students)

Four-Resources Model

The four-resources model by Allan Luke and Peter Freebody was adapted to promote a set of strategies necessary for reading and comprehension.

1. Code Breaker: "How do I crack this code?"	
This involves being able to decode and encode language. It includes recognizing and being able to speak and write words and sentences. It incorporates phonics and the use of accurate spelling and grammar.	Examples » What does that word mean in this context? » Which colours have been used in this picture?
2. Text Participant: "What does this mean, and what do I have to do to make it meaningful?"	
In the role of text participants, students use their knowledge of the world, knowledge of vocabulary, and knowledge of how language works to comprehend and compose texts.	Examples » Predict what you think this text is about. » Is this character like anyone that you know?
3. Text User: "What do I do with this text?"	
In this role, students are asked to think about how language varies according to context, purpose, audience, and content. They are required to apply this knowledge.	Examples » In what ways is this text similar to or different from others you have seen? » What special features does this text have?
4. Text Analyst: "What does this text do to me, and how?"	
By taking on this role, the students critically analyze and challenge the way texts are constructed to convey particular ideas and to influence people.	Examples » How is the composer of the text trying to make you feel and how is this accomplished? » Is the composer of this text being fair?

(Adapted from the online Tasmanian Department of Education Learning, Teaching, and Assessment Guide.)

By focusing on the four roles, the students are then able to practise the skills and processes that expert readers go through in the context of the text that is being read. Ultimately, the goal will be for the students to independently take on all of these roles — not in isolation — but in balance to strengthen comprehension and understanding.

Questions to develop the four strategies:

<table>
<tr><th colspan="2">Code Breaking</th></tr>
<tr><td>» How did you work out that difficult word?
» Which words are interesting?
» Which letter/s make that sound?
» Which other word might you use instead of this one?
» Which other words in this text have that sound?
» Which other words have that letter pattern?
» Is there another word here that has a similar meaning?</td><td>» What does that word mean in this context? Which other words come from the same base word?
» Which other words have the same prefix?
» Is the picture a close-up, medium shot, or long shot?
» Which colours have been used in this picture?
» What is happening in this image?
» What do you notice about the body language of the characters?</td></tr>
<tr><th colspan="2">Text Participating</th></tr>
<tr><td>» Predict what you think this text might be about.
» Does this text remind you of something that has happened to you?
» What did you feel as you read this text?
» What might happen next? Which words or phrases give you this idea?
» What would you do in this situation?
» How do you feel about the picture?</td><td>» What extra information does the picture give you?
» Is this character like anyone you know?
» What are the characters thinking or feeling?
» What might lie outside the frame of the picture?
» What do you think the next picture will look like?
» If you could ask the people in the picture a question, what would it be?</td></tr>
<tr><th colspan="2">Text Using</th></tr>
<tr><td>» What do you notice about the way this text looks?
» How is this text put together?
» Which special features does this text have?
» What is the purpose of this text?
» Which text type is this? How do you know?
» In what ways is this text like others you have read?
» In what ways is this text different from the last one we read?
» How can you find information in this text?
» If you wrote a text like this, what title would you give it?</td><td>» If you wrote a text like this, which words would you make sure you used?
» If you were going to put this text on the Web, what changes would you make?
» How would this text change if you were to use these ideas in a poem or a brochure or a poster?
» What title would you give this image?
» Who might have taken this picture? Where might it have come from?</td></tr>
<tr><th colspan="2">Text Analyzing</th></tr>
<tr><td>» What do you notice about the way this text looks?
» What opinions has the composer expressed? Why?
» What is fact and what is opinion in this text?
» What would the story be like if the main character were a girl instead of a boy? (or vice versa?)
» Whose story is or is not being told in the text? Why?
» Is the composer of this text being fair?
» In whose interest is this text?
» What do you notice about the types of words used most in this text?</td><td>» How is the composer of the text trying to make you feel? Why?
» How would this text be different if told in another place or time?
» Who does this text reject, silence, or marginalize?
» Why do you think the composer of the text included this image?
» What view of the world and values does the composer of this text assume that the reader or viewer holds? How do you know?
» How does this text construct a version of reality?
» How does this text use intertextuality to create its meaning?
» Having critically examined this text, what action are you going to take?</td></tr>
</table>

STRATEGY 30

Questioning the Author

The Questioning the Author (QTA) framework (McKeown, Beck & Worthy, 1993) can be helpful when used in the inquiry classroom. It helps students to achieve what is called an "authorial reading" by helping them to consider the "intelligence behind the text" — to think about who consciously composed the text — and uncover the messages that the author is communicating with the reader. QTAs start with initiating queries about the general topic and message, then follow up with queries that help students to think through elaborated meanings, including why and how the author constructed the message. Here is an example.

	Questioning the Author	
INITIATING QUERIES	1. What is the author trying to tell you?	
FOLLOW-UP QUERIES	2. Why is the author telling you that?	
	3. Does the author say it clearly?	
	4. How could the author have said things more clearly?	
	5. What would you say instead?	

In addition to the use of QTA and questioning prompts, we have found success in using "Bloom's Revised Taxonomy" as a basis to form questions to help students develop deeper understanding and engagement into the text. The students will gradually delve into more sophisticated forms of thinking from remembering, understanding, applying, analyzing, evaluating, and creating.

When doing a think aloud, you can promote authorial reading by asking:

- What does the author definitely want me to notice as I read? (Remembering)
- What are the key relationships (e.g., cause and effect) that the author wants me to perceive and understand? (Understanding)

» How can I use what I am learning here? In this context? In another context? (Applying)
» How can I connect the author's points here to other things I know or have learned? What patterns of meaning are emerging? (Analyzing)
» What is the author encouraging me to know, believe or do, why is that, and how do I feel about that? (Evaluating)
» What new perspective or understandings have I constructed as a result of conversing with this author's perspective? How has the author added to my capacity to make and/or perform ideas into actions as a result of my new understanding? (Creating)

These Bloom–QTA questions can be adapted for any subject area, e.g., in English for the reading of literary texts (see Buehl for applications to various other subject areas).

Questioning Taxonomy for Literary Texts

LEVEL OF THINKING	COMPREHENSION STATEMENT	FOCUSING QUESTION
Remembering	I can follow what happens in the story.	Who are the characters? Where does the story take place? What is the central conflict? What are the major events?
Understanding	I can understand what the author is communicating.	How is the author expressing conflict? What is the topic of the conflict? How do character relationships and interactions impinge on the topic? How does the setting constrain or encourage character action? How are major events related and connected?
Applying	I can use my understanding in meaningful ways.	How can I connect this story to my own life and experiences? How does the author use setting to affect characters? How can I use what I am learning in my own writing and thinking?
Analyzing	I can see new patterns of implied meaning and see how these were constructed and communicated. I can connect the dots of disparate ideas and events.	What implied relationships of ideas and events are expressed throughout the story? What literary devices and techniques are used to shape meaning?
Evaluating	I can critically examine and review the construction of this story and the intelligence behind the text.	What do the author's choices indicate about her attitude, perspective, etc.?
Creating	I have developed my own interpretation of what this story means. I can extend ideas and create new ideas and put them into actions based on my transaction with this text.	Why is the author telling this story? What generalization is the author expressing about life? How can I use/share/perform this new understanding in my own life and dealings with the world?

(Based on ideas from Doug Buehl, 2008)

Role Playing and Questioning

Having students ask questions whilst in role of a character is an excellent way of promoting deeper meaning and connections. We will explore this further in the next section on drama and visualization strategies, but here is an example of a questioning technique that can be used in role as a tool to uncover text meaning. The roles below are adapted from Morgan and Saxton (2006).

Students can select a card from a basket or just be given one. They must take on the role stated on the card that they selected. This can be a full-blown role play or done in small groups.

Examples: Roles that will promote questioning

The Absentee:

Questioner is aiming to fill in the blanks.

The Researcher:

Questioner is looking for something specific.

The Detective:

Questioner is looking for clues and patterns. The questions are indirect and divergent with the aim of drawing out information.

The Learner:

Questioner has a thirst for knowledge.

The Policeman:

Questioner is looking for facts; questions are direct.

The Interviewer:

Questioner is building a profile of the interviewee.

The Devil's Advocate:

Questioner is challenging the argument, statements, or the story by taking the opposite point of view.

As with all strategies, these can be adapted. The important thing for the teacher to look at is how will the questioning process help the student discover, understand, and make meaning as well as how will the outcome help the teacher learn about the student's thinking.

When developing questioning strategies, think about ...

What is the purpose of the questioning strategy used? How have you used questioning to help students:

» deepen their understanding

» see cause and effect

» compare and contrast

» see contrasts

» see change and continuity

» see through other people's perspectives

» see the past

» see sequence

» describe

» reflect

How have you used questioning to help teachers:

» assess students' understanding

» internalize the questioning strategies themselves for further use

STRATEGIES FOR VISUALIZATION, ACTION, AND DRAMA

A principle of inquiry is that the inquirer uses all available resources that assist in addressing the question or problem at hand. One does not divide tools into math or science or literacy, but uses whatever is available that can help. Likewise, any text form or art form that can shed light and insight into the inquiry should be used by the teacher in the inquiry classroom.

Using a Variety of Texts

This is powerful for student inquirers because they become exposed to different kinds of texts including short texts such as newspaper articles, popular culture texts, visual texts and artwork, visually supported texts, multimedia texts, electronic texts, cartoons, songs, and much more. This helps them to see that the issue at hand is not just a school topic but is alive in the culture. The multiple modalities in many texts help them to use and understand the major ideas and tools through various representational means.

Our collaborative team working on freedom vs. security made use of all these kinds of texts and invited students to find textual comments from the newspapers and Internet on their inquiry and bring these to class. The team actively invited students to see connections out in the world and bring these materials in as a focus of study.

But beyond using different kinds of texts that use different modalities to represent and communicate meanings, it is important to engage student inquirers into using multiple modalities to explore, placehold, and represent their own understandings.

There are many ways to do this with electronic technologies, and various arts such as dance. Here, though, we will offer examples from visual art and drama-in-education (also known as "action strategies") and other text forms. However, there are hundreds of techniques that could be used for visualization, and hundreds more that use drama and action strategies. (For full treatments and multiple examples of various techniques, see Jeffrey D. Wilhelm's *Reading Is Seeing*, 2004 and *Deepening Comprehension with Action Strategies*, 2003.)

Picture Mapping

Picture maps aid students' ability to see patterns in the text and to use the text's structure to help them better comprehend the author's ideas and purpose. Representing their understanding visually gives students another method to think through the ideas in a text and represent it for others. When thinking about the main ideas and structures of a text, students must reflect on the ideas and return to the text to clarify their thoughts, greatly aiding comprehension.

Example: Visual Assist — Picture Mapping

This exercise is useful for identifying the topic of a story or article and pointing out key details for the topic. Analyzing those details and the pattern between them, we can then determine the central focus of the text.

The teacher will provide a model for you using a short text, for example, on metal detectors in schools.

Now, working in groups of four, read through the article. Using what we know about topics, determine the topic of the article and create a picture or symbol to represent that topic.

Next, find the key details about the topic and create a visual representation for each one. Be sure to pay attention to what often signifies key details, including:

- » The beginning and end of the article
- » New paragraphs
- » Change of focus to a different idea
- » Quotations
- » Article sub-headings

After you have drawn the topic of the article and the supporting key details and the pattern between them, determine the main idea or central focus those details are pointing out. Draw a single picture to illustrate this central focus statement.

Once you have the details and the topic represented visually, make sure the relationship between these things is also apparent. For example, in my picture map, I have tied everything together as a kind of timeline of the world. Find a way to connect the key details and main topic on your picture map in a way that makes sense for the article.

Be prepared to explain your picture map to another group in five minutes. Afterward, all students share their picture maps with the whole class.

STRATEGY 33 Picturing Themes

Dan Fisher, from the Foothills School of Arts and Sciences, worked on an inquiry unit with a Grade 6/7 class. The students wrote essays on questions they had developed about the novels they had read. After completing the essays, students were asked to create a visual image that captures the heart of a novel — its essence. Along with the visual, students were required to select a quotation or two to accompany the visual. The following are some visual examples from the class.

CLIFF

"My hunting hat really gave me quite a lot of protection in a way, but I got soaked anyway."

"I had this feeling that I'd never get to the other side of the street. I thought I'd just go down, down, down and nobody'd ever see me again."

CAROUSEL

In this watercolour painting, the students place the carousel in the centre of a field of rye. Notice the red hunting cap at the bottom left of the picture.

"She went and got on the carousel. She walked all the way around if you know what I mean. She walked once all around it then she sat down on this big, brown beat up looking horse. Then the carousel started, and I watched her go around and around. There were only five or six other kids on the ride, and the song the carousel was playing was 'Smoke Gets in Your Eyes.'"

CATCHER IN THE RYE

"I'd just be the catcher in the rye."

THE OUTSIDERS

Students were told to select a central image from each chapter of the novel *The Outsiders* and place the images in chronological order around the hub of a wheel. Students then drew one image in the hub of the wheel to capture the essence of the entire novel.

A student created these visual tableaux, using a few key scenes or images to show the trajectory of the story. The student used some wood modelling figures from the art class to pose his characters for each chapter. He wanted to do something unique for his assignment.

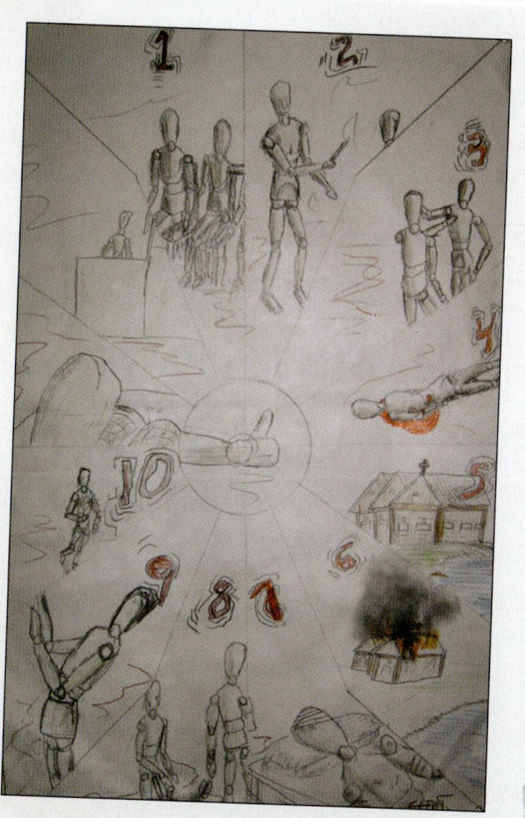

A key component of the story-mapping strategy is to have students share and articulate their picture maps with others.

Just as there are many different kinds of visual techniques that can help students to comprehend, placehold, represent, play with, and analyze what they are learning, so are there many drama and action strategies.

Hot Seating

Hot seating is a drama technique that puts students on the spot — in the hot seat. Whilst sitting in the hot seat, the students assume the role of a character other than themselves. They talk from the character's perspective and answer questions whilst in the role of the character. Below is a template that can be used to prepare students to take on the role of a character from a text being studied or pursued as part of a larger inquiry.

Hot Seating

Title of assigned reading: ______________________

In groups of 3-4 students, choose a character from this story that one of you will become for the hot seat. It is important that the group agree on the following information about the character so that any one of you could go to the hot seat and answer questions from the class. If the required information is not in the story, you will have to infer or make an educated guess about it.

Name of character: ______________________

Your age and physical appearance: ______________________

Your house, city/area, favourite place: ______________________

Your passions, "soap box" topics, deepest desires (these may not be mentioned in the text): ______________________

____

Your main goal: ______________________

____

Your biggest obstacles and problems: ______________________

____

Your biggest influences: ______________________

____

Your greatest strengths: ______________________

____

Your greatest weaknesses: ______________________

____

What one or two words best describe you – give examples from the text that demonstrate these traits: ______________________

____

-1-

Members of your group not being hot seated will get to ask the first two questions. What will they be? And how will your character respond? How do you know that these responses are good ones? ______________________________

____

Question 1: ______________________________

____

Answer: ______________________________

____

Question 2: ______________________________

____

Answer: ______________________________

____

What other questions might the audience ask? What will they want to know? How will your character respond and why will he/she respond that way? __________

____

____

–2–

(From *Action Strategies for Deepening Comprehension*, Wilhelm, 2002)

Variations on Hot Seating

Each student-in-role could have their "deep thoughts," "alter ego," or "conscience" stand behind them to reveal the inner thoughts and feelings that the character in the hot seat would not reveal in public. In this way, the student says what the character would say, but the alter ego says what the character might be thinking and feeling behind the persona or "mask." Review with your group what went well and what answers you would change.

Sequencing Drama Strategies

STRATEGY 35

Teachers have utilized drama strategies to foster deeper student understanding. In the following teaching example, teacher Josh Hale makes use of a variety of drama strategies in order to frontload, to consider personal school situations, to make connections from personal life to the story, to enter various perspectives, to discuss in ways that brought together the text, other texts, and the world to bear on the question, then to reflect on the story and the topic, and to practise writing mini-arguments. The example captures the teacher's summary and reflection of the process.

Lesson topic:

ROLES: Students cast as undercover officers who had just spent four months in local middle schools.

TEACHER IN ROLE: Chief of police called by the principals with concerns about bullying. They wanted these undercover officers in to help identify the types of bullying that was going on in their schools.

SET UP/FRAMING: Teacher informed students that their job was first to identify times, places, and situations where bullying occurs and then report out. Then they were also to identify causes and possible solutions to bullying given what they had observed about perpetrators and victims.

TECHNIQUE: Pairing and forum drama. In role as undercover officers, student pairs discussed what they had observed as officers (but really were using their own life experiences). The discussion produced a list of kinds of bullying, possible causes of bullying, and possible solutions to each type. Students could be asked to work in pairs or small groups to produce a report and proposal for the principal and teachers of the school.

TEACHER COMMENT: These students (officers) came up with the most amazing comments (of course). Because they were speaking as someone else, about unnamed people, their answers were right on. Because I was commenting as their senior officer, and not as their teacher, there was no concern of being punished or accused of any guilt.

NEXT STEPS: Class read the short story "Priscilla and the Wimps" by Richard Peck. As we read, we circled examples of bullying. Teacher modelled thinking aloud and responding, and identified issues related to bullying for the first half of the story, and then student pairs finished it on their own.

ASSESSMENT: I've read this story before with students. They usually laugh at the ending. Not this time!

Follow up technique: Radio Show

FRAMING: Students say they would do a call-in radio show discussion about bullying. They are each to choose a role from the story, literature, movies, or from history, our unit, or popular culture — but it must be a person or character who has very strong perspectives and feelings about bullying. They are not allowed to be themselves, and must identify who they are and where they are from when they call in to the show.

SET UP: Students work in pairs brainstorming who they might want to be and what that person would say about the situation in the story and bullying in general and what to do about it.

SMALL GROUPS: In groups of six, one student acts as host and other group members call in to have their say. Participants must be in role of someone in history, popular culture, or literature read prior to this reading. They would have strong feelings about the issue. Participants can be asked to "uptake" or use a prior speaker's comments — agreeing, extending, adapting, or disagreeing — to encourage true dialogue and building of meaning.

Whole Class Discussion:

TEACHER IN ROLE: The talk show host.

PROCESS: Teacher began by saying that our community is very concerned about the bullying going on in our community. Poor Monk Klutter (the bully in the story) was found stuffed in his locker after being trapped there for a week. Teacher encouraged people who were also concerned about the bullying to call in.

ASSESSMENT: The students again were awesome. Priscilla (the one who bullied the bully) called in. Priscilla's mom called in. Melvin, members of Klutter's Kobras, and Monk himself called in.

So did "Martin Luther King," "Sigmund Freud," "Little Mermaid," Weena (from *The Time Machine*), "Oprah Winfrey," and "Dr. Phil." Very eye-opening, very involving. Many new connections were made. The students said things in role that they would not say as themselves, and they made connections and responded to each other in ways rarely seen in a regular discussion.

FOLLOW UP WRITING: From there we took off to an informal exploratory writing assignment where students answered the question "Who's the bully in 'Priscilla and the Wimps'?" They were incredibly motivated to write; they had all their data and examples circled. They were ready with warrants and explanations to support their claims. They also responded to what they knew would be other students' objections so they learned to respond to reservations. This really helped them to prepare for our final argument paper. We used these mini-arguments as the basis for a debate.

Afterward I asked students what they thought about these new strategies. Some students commented: "You had to participate." "Even if you participated less than other kids, you were still totally involved." "It was very motivating." "We [the students] did all the work." "We did a better job on the writing because of the acting out." "It made us learn more."

As an extension, I would suggest a culminating project in which the students will use all of what they have learned throughout the unit and apply it to our school to create a Student Information Guide about bullying.

STRATEGY 36

Panel Discussion

Another kind of discussion drama is a panel discussion or debate where students take on the roles of characters, authors, or historical figures from their inquiry. Here's one from the freedom vs. security unit for the novel *1984*.

Please attend a PANEL DISCUSSION

TOPIC:
"Balance Between Freedom and Security"

GUEST SPEAKERS INCLUDE:
Winston Smith, Julia, O'Brien, Mr. Parsons, Symes, and Emmanuel Goldstein

***Please come to class prepared to role play one of the characters in the novel. Consider their individual perspectives regarding the importance of both Freedom and Security and whether or not each character would endorse a balance between the two, and what that would be like, or the elimination of one or the other. If you are not participating in the panel discussion as one of the main characters, you will have the opportunity to ask questions of one of the esteemed speakers.*

Participants will be asked to respond in role to the following statements — giving and supporting their opinion.

1. Governing bodies act in the best interest of the people.
2. People should never compromise their ideals or beliefs.
3. In some instances, violence is acceptable.
4. Rules are necessary.
5. Freedom means doing whatever you want.
6. Hidden cameras are a violation of my right to privacy.
7. People suspected of a crime are innocent until proven guilty.
8. Civil rights should apply equally to all people.
9. It is possible that other people know what's best for me.
10. Children should have special rights and/or protections.
11. Those who have been marginalized or who are underprivileged should have special rights.

How would each character respond to each of the statements? You should be able to cite specific examples from the text that backs your statements while role-playing the characters. For example, in the meeting with O'Brien, both Winston and Julia promise to take whatever action necessary to help further the cause of the Brotherhood. They even promise to kill babies if need be! I think that qualifies as agreeing with "In some instances, violence is acceptable." (#3). Also, when participating in the panel discussion, remember physical mannerisms that the characters possess. It seems like I remember something about the way O'Brien adjusts his glasses and Winston has some sort of ailment in his ankle. What other mannerisms could you represent while portraying one of the characters?

We've already alluded to the importance of using a variety of multiple modalities in the texts you read in a unit. It's also important to use a variety of text types, from children's and young adult literature to popular culture, which exhibit varying levels of challenge and various kinds of genres and text structures: narrative, exposition, explanation, definition, classification, and various kinds of argument.

Quoting experts, interviewing, or conversing with experts (personally, through text, or through drama) can highlight the ways of thinking and justifying thought that different experts use. It can also foreground different perspectives and areas of disagreement around the inquiry question.

It is useful to use short pieces that connect in various ways and that can be put into conversation with each other. In this way students are invited to see multiple perspectives and complexity, and are invited to make decisions of their own, instead of playing "guess what the teacher already knows" or thinks.

Using short texts that exhibit the same conventions and structures gives students the requisite practice to develop familiarity and facilitates reading and writing that text type. This promotes the all-important sense of self-efficacy and competence discussed in an earlier section.

Besides simply choosing texts that provide variety in terms of structure and perspective, teachers can work to help students see things from other points of view. The best way we know to do this is to use what Deborah Appleman (1999) calls "critical lenses" to challenge and shift students' perspectives, and give them a way to see and understand ideas they could not understand from their previous thinking and positions.

STRATEGY 37 Critical Thinking Lens

In the inquiry classroom, teachers can use a critical theory lens to read, interpret, or critique at least one text as part of the unit. This could include a popular culture text (song lyrics, advertisement, MTV video, TV show, movie, etc.)

- This could be the power lens that helps us to see issues of power (cf. Marxism)
- The gender lens that helps us to see issues of gender (cf. Feminism)
- The authorial reading lens that helps us to understand the author and what is expected from us as readers
- The cultural lens that helps us see from a different culture or time period
- The reader response lens that helps us identify and explore our own perspective

When designing a critical lens assignment, the assignment should help students to understand the lens and its uses, to understand and use the lens with a particular text, and how to use the lens with other texts and world situations. The assignment should serve the purpose of reading and understanding the text(s) at hand ***in a new way***, i.e., the students should be helped to read and understand in a way that they would not normally read. The use of the lens should help the students to see the world in a new way, and learn new ways of acting or being in the world. For full discussions of these critical theories and how to use them, we suggest reading Deborah Appleman's (1999) *Critical Encounters in High School English*.

The following is a sequence of learning experiences where the teaching team, in the Freedom vs. Security Unit, have framed learning using the critical lens theory.

INTRODUCTION:
There are a lot of different groups in this school and in each of our lives. Some groups have more security; some are able to exercise more freedom and privilege than others. How and why does this happen and what might we do about it? To explore this, make a list of the groups either in this school or in your everyday life. Now rank them from first to last of who has the most power, who is the most popular, or who is the most successful.

Experimenting with the Power Lens

Let's explore how power and privilege are represented and explored in two popular movies.

Examples:

1. Julia Roberts in the movie *Pretty Woman* walks into a boutique store in Rodeo Drive and the shop assistant assumes she cannot afford the clothing based on what she is wearing.
2. In *Maid in Manhattan,* Jennifer Lopez's character tries on the clothing of one of the wealthy hotel guests and when sighted by another wealthy guest is assumed to be wealthy and part of the social elite.

CLASS DISCUSSION:

- Why did the characters react in the way they did?
- What was the hierachy represented in the two movies?

SMALL GROUP DISCUSSION:
Discuss a specific situation in which someone treated you differently (positively or negatively) because of your economic standing or other reasons.

Example:
When I was a sophomore in college my friends and I jumped in a van and drove down the Oregon coast, through California and to San Francisco. We slept on the beach, nine of us in a single tent. The next morning we drove into the city and spent all morning and afternoon at the pier and in Chinatown. Most of us hadn't showered in a few days, hadn't shaved in a week and were wearing clothes dirtied from hiking, playing on the sand and driving in our sweaty vehicle. When it began to get dark, we started to wander around the city, which eventually led us into the more well-to-do part of town with its expensive stores, corporations, and swanky apartment buildings towering above us as we watched people walk in and out of restaurants and nightclubs. We thought it might be fun to look at the expensive clothes in one of the particularly nice boutiques. When we walked inside, the reaction of the people working there was humorous, albeit slightly depressing; we were completely ignored. I was wearing tennis shoes that had been in the ocean earlier that day, a jacket that had seen the worst of Oregon's spontaneous weather, and a thick wool beanie. As we stood there, rifling through the shirts, pants, and sweaters, comparing prices in quiet disbelief, a woman, obviously upper class, came in with her daughter, her style akin to that of Paris Hilton. Before the door could swing shut, two of the women working were by her side, offering all of the assistance a person could ask for. We walked back out into the night, laughing at the small injustice that we had just been a part of.

INFORMAL WRITING:
Compose a short freewrite/journal entry about a time when you or someone else was treated in a particular way, perhaps preferentially or unfairly, because of perceptions of status and power.

FOLLOW UP:
How does the situation you've created relate to our inquiry question? Consider who feels most secure, what determines who is a "have" or a "have-not." Who had the most power? What kind of power does each group have? How does status and power affect freedom and security or the lack of it?

APPLICATION TO READING:
List all of the characters in your freedon vs. security journal. Now create a ladder with the most powerful character on the top, and put characters in order down to the lowest rung. Who will be the character with the least power? The most power? What point is the author making through who is portrayed as having power and not having power?

SMALL GROUP DISCUSSION:
What point is made by this hierarchy? What are the costs and benefits to the characters and this hierarchy to their society? Are there any possibilities for upending the hierarchy or helping certain characters climb up the ladder? What will be the challenges to doing so?

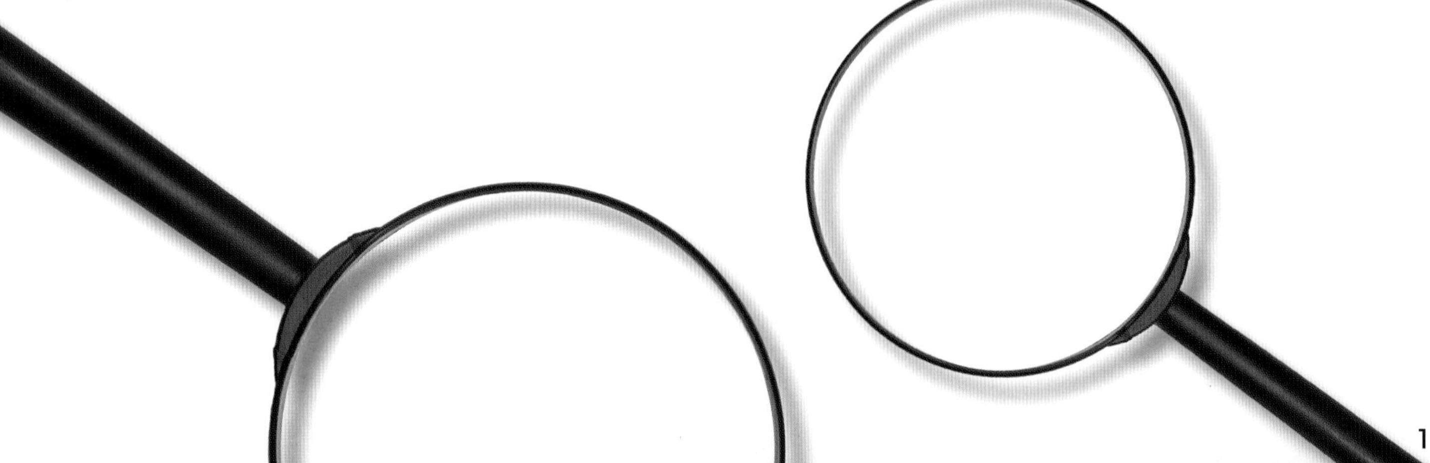

Low-Key Drama

This example of framing a low key drama was presented to a group of Tasmanian teachers by Dr. Norah Morgan based on the work of Jonothan Neelands in the book, *Asking Better Questions*.

Take a small fragment of prose or a poem with lots of unanswered questions. See the following example:

"In the year AD 2020 Mary Ellery, daughter of William and Elizabeth Ellery, left her home in Townsville to travel to the planet Osiris. She was a member of the group 'Venture' led by Doctor James Harvey. Mary never returned though she had left earth with the group. The team does not speak of her. There is no mention of her in the records and her name does not appear in the medal citation which honors the work of Dr. Harvey and his group."

The teacher explains that the class will be creating a group story where everyone must listen to the ideas and suggestions of the members and not impose his or her story on the group.

The teacher puts the fragment on the board and asks: What do we know? (facts only) These are written up.

The teacher asks groups of 4/5 with craft paper and felt pens: "What do we need to know to enrich the story?"

The students are allowed five questions per group. Limiting the number ensures that students will avoid one-word answers. The teacher might find it useful to let the class decide as a group what is Mary's age or wait until later. Allow 5-7 minutes for this. The questions are written on the paper provided.

The lists are shared, discussed, criticized until all groups are satisfied! The questions are placed where all can see them.

The teacher then asks: "Who might be able to answer those questions?" Names are listed on the board. Limit the number to about eight names (e.g., parents, Harvey, Mary's friends/colleagues). Mary cannot be questioned as she did not return.

The teacher then asks for four volunteers to take on the role of the people listed. While the volunteers are deciding whom they will represent, the class is put into role as people who are interested in solving the disappearance of Mary Ellery.

ALL ARE INFORMED THAT IT IS NOW AD 2030.

The teacher arranges four chairs facing North, South, East, and West. Those to be interviewed come one at a time and those awaiting their turn must listen as they cannot change what previous information has been revealed.

The teacher warns the group that, as it is 10 years later, some things may be have been forgotten. Some may be classified information, some may be too painful to reveal, and we must respect those who have agreed to answer our questions.

The teacher usually asks the first question in a low-key role and then the class takes over the questions. When all have been interviewed, the class may ask questions of whom they wish.

The group reassembles and shares what new information they now have. The teacher could ask students to bring to the next class an artifact that might open the case still further (letter, will, object) and share these before each student writes his/her account of the mystery. The questions asked can be recorded and analyzed.

When designing visualization, action, and drama strategies, think about ...

- » Each activity should require students to evoke the world of the text.
- » The activities should encourage students to elaborate on the story world, to fill in gaps, to make inferences, and to extend their reading beyond the text.
- » The activities should encourage students to revisit textual facts and details and experiences, and to re-organize, bring forward, and reflect upon what they learned.
- » The activities should encourage students to achieve a richer and more "valid" reading of the text.
- » The activities should ask students to hone other skills such as interviewing skills, news show formats, review writing, etc.
- » The activities should be fun for the kids, and should ask students to learn something they didn't already know (instead of just revisiting what they already know) and to achieve or practice some new learning processes they do not already master.
- » The activities should do some real-world work, a community service or partner school project, etc.

STRATEGIES FOR DIFFERENTIATION/LAYERING

The previous section on Visualization, Action, and Drama strategies highlighted the importance of providing students with a number of different modalities for learning. From these strategies and the following, we believe it is important to continually acknowledge that with any group of students, at any age, there are varying abilities. Inquiry fits naturally into layering or differentiating activities to meet all students' needs. It doesn't require teachers to create numerous plans for each level that the students are operating at, but rather to have activities that provide choice and direction for the different students' abilities and acknowledge the different entry points that students will have in the learning. Because inquiry is all about meeting students where they are and then moving them to a new level of understanding, the layering of activities is essential. Students need the opportunities to practise and grapple with the procedural skills in a variety of different ways. Students move forward and progress from a process of working together through teacher guidance, being stretched by peers, and through individual practice and ownership of their own learning (refer to scaffolding through inquiry diagram on page 52).

The chart below shows the differences between traditional and differentiated instruction.

Differentiated curriculum is:	Differentiated curriculum is not:
» having high expectations for all students	» individualization; it isn't a different lesson plan for each student each day
» providing multiple assignments within each unit, tailored for students with differing levels of achievement	» giving all students the same work most of the time
» allowing student to choose, with the teacher's guidance, ways to learn and how to demonstrate what they have learned	» spending significant amounts of time teaching material they have mastered to others who have not mastered it
» permitting students to demonstrate mastery of material they already know and to progress at their own pace through new material	» assigning more work at the same level to high achieving students
» structuring class assignments so they require high levels of critical thinking but permit a range of responses	» all the time; often it is preferable for students to work as a whole class
» assigning activities geared to different learning styles, interests, and levels of thinking and achievement	» grouping students into co-operative learning groups that do not provide for individual accountability or do not focus on work that is new to all students
» providing students with choices about what and how they learn	» using only the differences in student responses to the same class assignment to provide differentiation
» flexible; teachers move students in and out of groups based upon students' instructional needs	» limited to acceleration; teachers are encouraged to use a variety of strategies

(From Tomlinson, C.A. and Allan, 2000. *Leadership for Differentiating Schools and Classrooms*, Alexandria, VA: Association for Supervision and Curriculum Development)

Layering activities can be done in many ways. Here are a few strategies that students can use in different ways that are appropriate to their current interests and capacities. Although responses will differ, they will still add to understanding the inquiry topic and allow students to contribute to the common inquiry project in their own way.

- Varied texts
- Discussion and activity cubes
- Literature circles
- Discovery circles
- Varied journal prompts
- Questioning strategies
- Role playing
- Compacting
- Tic-Tac-Toe
- Discussion cards
- RAFTS

Role, Audience, Format, Topic (RAFT)

RAFTs "frame and organize students' exploratory writing by articulating different aspects of any rhetorical situation for writing" and encourage creative responses for all students. You may organize these to help with point of view, writing across the curriculum, and layering. You can have student choice in which students pick one item from each column (as below) or you may simply assign the role, audience, form, and topic. Students will have the opportunity to show their creativity.

Role	Audience	Form	Topic
Sidney Crosby	Friend	Love letter	War in Afghanistan
Oprah Winfrey	Stalker fan	Thank you note	Poverty in Africa
Angelina Jolie	Publicist	Persuasive letter	An appearance on a talk show
Barack Obama	Public	Complaint	Censorship

Choice Centres

Choice centres allow student or teacher choices. There are a variety of activities providing different modalities and different levels of responses that help students investigate topics further. These centres can be adapted for drama, writing, reading, technology, viewing, and experimenting.

There are many examples of how these can be used but they especially work well as a reading response. Following Bloom's Taxonomy, teachers may create their own choice centres that use the different questioning verbs and/or learning modalities. After reading *The 10 Grossest Bugs* (Scholastic Canada), students might choose one activity from the following choice board.

Create a web that demonstrates the characteristics of "gross" bugs.	Compare and contrast two of your favourite bugs using a Venn diagram.	Design and draw your own bug and describe the characteristics that make it weird.
Create a skit with two other students to demonstrate a conversation between two of these bugs and how they survive.	**FREE CHOICE**	Write a journal entry from the perspective of one of these bugs describing a typical day.
Create a comic strip to show how one bug hides through camouflage in the wild.	Make up a rap about the most adaptable bug in this book. Tell it from the bug's point of view about the world.	Create an online search for other gross bugs.

Tic-Tac-Toe

The Tic-Tac-Toe is a modified version of a choice centre. Students choose one activity in each row to form a straight line either horizontally, vertically, or diagonally, allowing layering opportunities as well as student choice. In this case, there is student choice but also guaranteed accountability that a set number of tasks will be completed that vary in modality.

Write about the main character of your story including physical description, personality traits, and other interesting politics. Share with your neighbour.	In your journal, create a graphic organizer and use it to compare yourself to the main character.	Think of someone you know who is like one of the characters in the book. Write about how they are alike.
Draw a picture of the setting of the story.	Make a rap about the setting of the story and set it to music.	Build a model of the setting of the story.
Create a timeline that shows the major events in this story.	Create a storyboard that represents a scene from your book. With characters that you create, describe and act out the scene.	Create a skit with three other students that demonstrates a new ending to this story.

Discussion Cube

STRATEGY 42

A discussion cube allows students to examine an issue from a variety of perspectives, different levels of questioning, and/or layering of responses. The idea is presented in Carol Tomlinson's work together with the use of Bloom's Taxonomy to guarantee different levelling of questioning. As well, different groups can be given different cubes that prompt different kinds of work, levels of questions or responses, etc. These cubes can be colour-coded for ease of use. This allows for differentiation, or different responses for various texts read in the class. The students roll the cube like a die and complete the task on the face that lands side up.

Discussion Cube Templates

As a discussion prompt in the context of "freedom vs. security," teachers showed a short video dramatization about "thinking before you post." Examples of videos around the issues of privacy and confidentiality could be used to get students to respond to a prompt like: How can you avoid some of the dangers of the Internet?

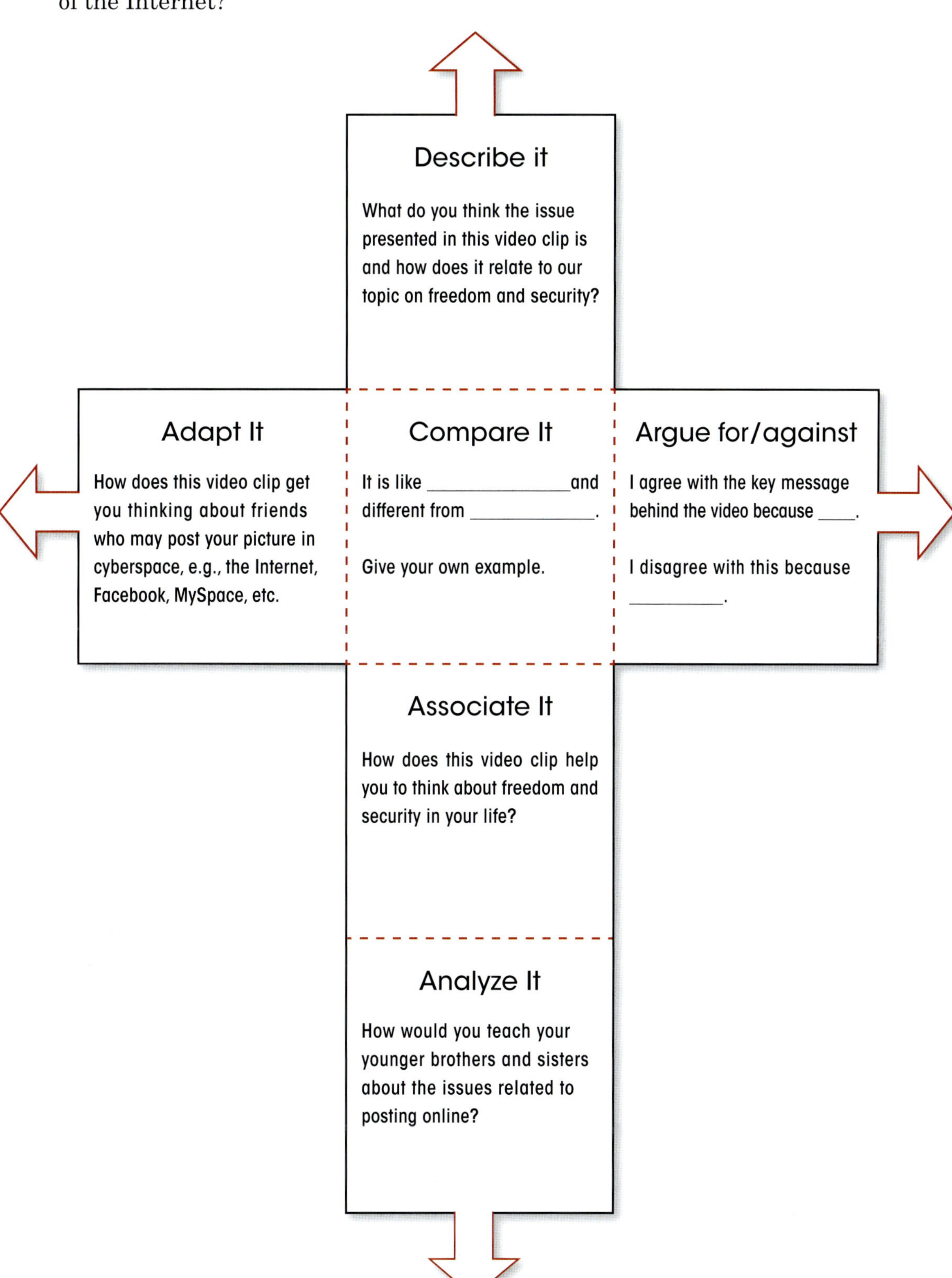

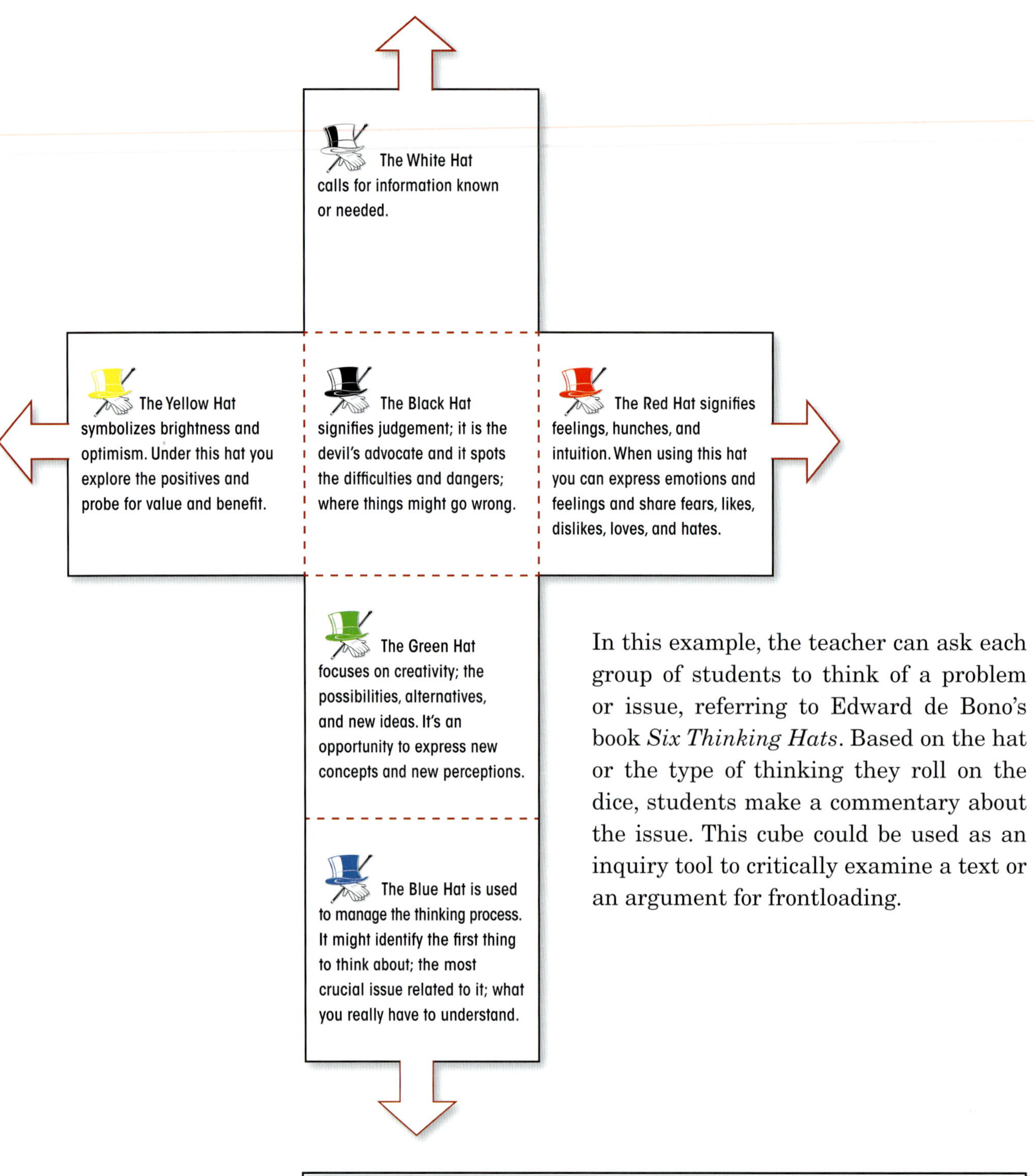

In this example, the teacher can ask each group of students to think of a problem or issue, referring to Edward de Bono's book *Six Thinking Hats*. Based on the hat or the type of thinking they roll on the dice, students make a commentary about the issue. This cube could be used as an inquiry tool to critically examine a text or an argument for frontloading.

When designing layered activities, think about...

- Tweaking activities to meet a variety of students' needs
- Layering activities to different modes and entry levels, for example, through use of Bloom's Taxonomy, de Bono's thinking hats, etc.
- Providing students with choice in completing projects
- Using learning centres in the classroom
- Allowing for flexible groupings

STRATEGIES FOR FORMATIVE ASSESSMENT

It is especially important for students learning something new and challenging to get continuous feedback and visible signs of progress and accomplishment. Often we wait and provide relatively few assessments that are high stakes — in the form of tests or long writing assignments.

Our contention is that we would do much better and our students would be much more successful if we continuously, on a daily basis, provide helpful feedback and "formative" assessment, i.e., assessment that would inform our instruction, and focus students on areas of strengths to build on, as well as areas for more practice and improvement. This formative feedback would name students as readers, writers, and problem solvers and would name their capacities as well as what they could do next to develop these capacities. This would highlight student strengths instead of deficits, and would provide the kind of motivation that comes from developing and desiring continuously improving competence.

We believe that all of the activities mentioned in the book so far not only offer rich possibilities for instructing, assisting, and supporting students to understand new concepts and processes, but also ways for students to make visible what they already know and are learning. When teachers pay attention to what students produce in a frontloading discussion, a classroom drama, debate, or informal writing, we can learn from our students what they know and can do, and what we can do next to help them on the journey toward more expertise.

It's also important to allow students time and supportive structures for naming and self-monitoring their own progress. By using strategies for reflection, students are allowed time to reflect, monitor, and track their thinking and skills development within the unit. Teachers are able to see the connection and developments in student thinking and students are able to articulate and name their own critical standards and their growth toward these.

Metacognition Stems

Metacognition Stems are one technique that is quick and informative, and can be done in a variety of ways to fit the needs of your students. Metacognition stems can be used through the following strategies and adapted easily to your topic of study.

» Sticky notes
» Exit ticket
» Entrance pass
» Portfolio reflection
» Journal entry
» Letter
» Index cards that are kept in a box

Examples of metacognition stems

» The thing that surprised me the most today was ...
» One thing I am confused about is ...
» How do I ...
» One thing I learned and do not want to forget is ...
» As a result of today's class, I will now ...
» This reminds me of ...
» I want to learn more about ...
» One thing I learned today that connected with something I knew before was ...

Teachers can easily develop specific stems that are based upon the content of your lesson:

Examples:
» One place where I might use this kind of algebra in my everyday life is ...
» Two examples of an animal's habitat are ...
» My favourite art technique is ... because ...

Although all of the activities in this book can be used to track progress and make learning visible, here are a few easier activities. These activities help to give insight into how an activity helped students in their understandings.

Place Markers

PLACE MARKERS

Name: ______________________

I want to remember:

____

____

____

____

____

Place markers can be used to help students remember where they are in their thinking. For example, students can remember where they are in their learning, a particular part of the book, a point left off in a small group discussion, etc. We keep a pile of these bookmark types of paper in the classroom so that at a moment's notice we can ask students to use them.

For example, students can record an important insight, something to remember, a stimulus for getting started the next day, an idea to research, a goal to pursue next, etc. Such markers can be created by the teacher for various purposes and made available to students, or students can create their own based on the teacher's suggestions or on their own current needs.

Exit Tickets and Entrance Tickets

EXIT TICKET

Name: ______________________

What is the most important thing I learned about the country's security today and how does it affect my life?

____

____

____

____

Exit tickets and entrance tickets get at the same issues, and are collected at the end of class, or at the beginning of the next class. This provides data about what students know and areas of challenge we might need to help them through.

Exit tickets are used in the same way. Again, a pile of these may be kept in the classroom so that we can easily have students fill one out at the end of an activity. Or students can compose their own exit tickets on notebook paper from a prompt on the board. For the entrance tickets, students need to come to class with an assigned reflection in order to "get in" to class. It might be a self-reflection or a response to the previous lesson and takes the same format as exit tickets.

3-2-1 Bridge

The 3-2-1 Bridge can be a useful strategy for activating prior knowledge, reflecting on learning in a lesson or activity, making connections, and naming or demonstrating understanding. In its simplest form, students can be asked to write down three words/thoughts/ideas; two questions; and one analogy/metaphor/crucial idea/definition/application depending on the purpose and substance of the lesson. The students can be asked to write down their initial responses to the topic or question in this manner and then later add what their new responses are. The 3-2-1 Bridge becomes a way of tracing how their new understandings emerge from their original responses. As you can see, the students are asked to uncover their initial thoughts and understandings and then shift the thinking to a new deeper understanding.

	Name:
3	Things I found interesting ...
2	Lingering questions or wonderings or things that I want to explore more in the future ...
1	Goal that I have for my learning for next lesson ...

The 3-2-1 Bridge strategy can be used with any reader in an inquiry unit. Start off by stating the essential question.

Essential Question:			
Initial Responses to the Question		New Responses to the Question	
3	Words/Thoughts/Ideas	3	Words/Thoughts/Ideas
2	Questions	2	Questions
1	Analogy/Metaphor/Connection	1	Analogy/Metaphor/Connection

Muddy/Marvy Moments

Muddy and "marvy" moments is a technique that students record both something they are still confused about and something that was really interesting. Students write their muddy and/or marvy moments on a sticky note, placing them on the wall as they leave class, giving teachers an "at a glance" assessment as well as highlights categories to focus on or issues to be addressed through further teaching and learning. The strategy also allows for a celebration of the successes (marvellous moments) that have been achieved.

In a Grade 3 class, students responded to a frontloading activity on "What is culture?" Students wrote either or both a muddy moment and a marvy moment on a sticky note and added their initials. With just a quick look, teachers were able to gain insight into how the students were thinking. Teachers then tracked the students' understanding throughout the unit as they explored the meaning of culture in their own lives, school life, and in the broader community. Each day of the unit, the student responses informed their teachers' instructional planning for the next day and allowed them to learn from their students how to teach them more effectively.

Marvellous Moments	Muddy Moments
» I understand how dancing expresses culture and important stories. » I understand cultures by asking questions about other people's cultures. » I understand American language. » I understand people dance at celebrations and parties in different cultures and they have different dance moves. » I understand what they mean by sports. » I know everybody has a different culture — even in our own classroom. » I would like to see everybody's culture. » I understand American food culture, such as eating hamburgers. » Part of American culture is electricity. » I understand how we have different art forms. » I understand that art and language are part of culture. » I know languages are part of culture.	» How does the American culture react to money? » I don't understand what culture is. » What is heritage? » Why do we have different opinions if we share culture? » What do Mexican ideas about death have to do with their culture? » How is death treated in our culture? » What does how is "death treated" mean? » How are foods a part of culture? » How do you study culture? » What is a daily schedule? » I don't understand all the languages. » I don't understand the Mexican language. » How does being born describe culture?

Where Are You Sailing?

This is another technique to help students reflect on where they are on the continuum of understanding. At various times in the unit, they can be asked to identify what concepts and strategies they do not yet feel competent to use (in harbour), which ones they could use with help and support from a teacher (leaving port), conceptual and strategic tools they can use with a peer (approaching open waters), and those they can use independently (sailing high seas).

Students can be asked to not only name what their perceived level of mastery and independence of various central concepts and procedures are, but to provide some indication or evidence of why they see themselves being where they are. They could even offer suggestions regarding the help or opportunities that they think would help them grow or consolidate their competence. Reflecting and naming such things is important to metacognitive awareness and self-regulation in learning and is well worth the time, effort, and even struggle that might be involved.

Still in Harbour	Leaving Port
Approaching Open Waters	**Sailing High Seas**

STRATEGY 49

Student-Designed Rubrics

Inquiry helps students name what makes a good learner and what makes a good product. Giving students the opportunity to help set the criteria for a project not only gives them personal investment but also allows them to name the "what" and the "how" of a good artifact. As teachers we have our own rubric or criteria in mind. It is important that we share and even negotiate this with our students prior to beginning a set task or learning experience. One way of achieving this is through classroom discussions or in small groups by actually having our students design what they think would make an excellent product (student-designed rubric). Then the class designs the rubric with teachers guiding the students through questioning to create a dynamic but complete rubric. Clear expectations give students the framework to create and show their learning in a way that they are invested in. With this investment, the students are more likely to actually produce a quality artifact.

The example on page 141 is a rubric designed by a Grade 9 music class at the Foothills School of Arts and Sciences. The culminating project was to create a radio show that exhibited the students' understanding of how the political and social culture in America was represented by the folk song ballads of the 1960s. The class brainstormed the criteria for the culminating project. Then they completed a Round Robin of these brainstormed categories (see grouping strategies for Round Robin). At the end, each group took one topic and made the final rubric for that category. It didn't take long and the students were totally invested in the criteria. In addition, they understood more deeply what makes a good project and artifact as well as how to undergo the process.

Student Interview

Students interview each other in pairs. Each student asks the other a set of questions and records the answers. Teachers can develop interview guides that are specific to the topic or use a generic interview form with these questions:

- Describe something new that you learned through this activity/ learning experience.
- Describe the process you went through as a learner.
- What supported your learning?
- What hindered your learning?
- What was important to you while you were learning?
- How did you know you had learned something?

Example: Culminating Media Project

CATEGORY/ CRITERIA	PROFESSIONAL	AMATEUR	RE-AUDITION	WHAT WAS I THINKING?
CONTENT: » Selected songs from chosen year » Main song writers » Historical events of the year » Political events » Key social events	» Content was outstanding. » Content was applicable and accurate to year of focus. » The radio play included at least three main song writers. » Included clear explanation of how and why the songs were important. » Clear connection to how the music reflected the historical, political, and key social events of the time.	» Content was very good. » Content was mostly applicable to the year of focus. » The radio play included at least two main song writers. » Included some explanation of why the songs were important. » Included some connection between the music and the historical, political, and social events of the time.	» Content was good but needed to be more specific as to how it linked to the year of focus. » The radio play included at least one main song writer. » Only barely touched upon why the songs were important. » A brief connection between the music and the historical, political, and social events of the time was included.	» Content was not applicable to the year of focus. » The radio play did not include main song writers or how they were influenced by the historical, political, and social events of that chosen year.
PARTS OF A RADIO SHOW: » Narration involving the content criteria » Additional material appropriate to their selected year (in the 60s) e.g., commercials, news spot, sports etc.	» Clear narration of the content criteria. » Lots of appropriate material was selected.	» Good narration of the content criteria. » Appropriate material was selected.	» Some narration included. » Some appropriate material selected.	» Little or no narration included. » Little or no appropriate material selected.
QUALITY OF PRODUCTION: » Transition » Clear diction and clarity of presentation » Thought and presentation » Balance of spoken text and audio » Sound effects used to enhance production	» Excellent transitions used. Smooth and professional. » Very clear diction, a professional sound was achieved. » Highly original and clever. » An excellent balance of spoken text and audio.	» Very good transitions used. » Very good diction used. » Some very good production features used. » A very good balance of spoken text and audio.	» Some good transitions were used. » Good diction but there were some parts that needed polish. » Production was good with some areas for polish. » Audio and spoken text was used with some areas in need of polish.	» The transitions were poor and/or non-existent. » The production was not clear and diction was difficult to decipher. » The production was choppy and/or unoriginal. » Little if no balance used — over dominance of one form.

STRATEGY 50

Portfolio Cover Sheet

It is important to track student learning and to involve students in assessing their own learning. Students can use a portfolio to collect evidence of their learning and compose cover sheets for their submissions. Teachers can also create cover sheets for student submissions. In this way, both students and teachers work together to tell the story of students' learning and to highlight the evidence.

Name of Work Sample:
Why I included it:
» It shows improvement and growth when I compare it to previous work and understanding by ... » It shows that I took a risk and tried something new by ... » It is something I could use as part of my culminating project if I would ... » It shows I have met one of the major unit goals for conceptual or procedural understanding. Name of goal ... » Other: I could extend or will use what I have learned from this work sample in the future by ...
Peer or parent comment on the work sample:
______________________________ ______________________________ ______________________________ ______________________________ ______________________________ ______________________________

A portfolio cover sheet can get at the reason for the submission, because it shows signs of: risk-taking, progress, meeting of certain learning goals, and best effort.

Teacher Portfolio Cover Sheet

Work Sample	What the work tells me about this student's understanding	What the work does not tell me about this student's understanding	Questions I could ask this student whilst conferring (to shed light on level of understanding)	Teaching move(s) I could make (increase student ability to make sense of text and demonstrate understanding)
1.				
2.				
3.				

Evidence of Understanding

The ultimate goal is for our students to be actively involved in the creation and maintenance of a portfolio of evidence of understanding. They first collect work samples, then select those work samples that demonstrate growth toward the meeting of unit goals. They would then reflect on and justify how certain selections show growth or the meeting of goals. Students then proceed to think about the real work they could do in the world, based on what they have learned.

When designing assessment tools, think about...

- What is it that I am assessing? What is the purpose of the activity or learning sequence?
- How will my students be showing me what they know?
- What procedural and conceptual knowledge are my students naming in this activity/learning sequence?
- How will my students be demonstrating their understanding?
- What opportunities will they have to demonstrate their understanding in new ways?
- How will the students leave this activity thinking about something in a new way or change in a new way?

CONCLUSION

Throughout this book, we have talked about various strategies that can help deepen student thinking and understanding. We have proposed that learning is most powerfully framed as an inquiry and that the most effective instruction is teaching with wide-awake intent. When we teach with intent, we are consciously framing and scaffolding every lesson and activity in a way that is connected to the controlling inquiry centre and is therefore clearly purposeful for our students and their progress toward the independent capacity to create a culminating project that stakes their identity, that expresses their thinking and understanding, and that is of use in the world.

This is the essence of inquiry-based learning. The teaching and the learning are intentional and guided by an essential question and sub-questions that in turn afford our students the time and focus to develop deeper understandings. Every strategy and technique is used to promote understanding and progress toward independent transfer and use of the central conceptual and procedural tools.

We have demonstrated that in order to teach for understanding, one must also plan and assess for understanding. This involves using activities in the classroom to foster collaboration and community and applying a variety of inquiry strategies to support learning. Learning, formative assessment, and demonstration of progress can be achieved through the use of strategies such as:

- frontloading
- reading and thinking aloud
- discussion
- questioning and connection making
- visualization, action, and drama
- layering and differentiation
- assessment strategies

The aim is to not use these strategies in isolation but in an intentional manner, asking ourselves: "What is the intent? How does this strategy fulfill our intent and do functional work in the context of the inquiry?"

Guidelines for Teaching With Intent

- What is the purpose of the activity I am having students do?
- How is this activity in service of the essential question and the big understandings for the whole unit?
- How is this activity differentiated and layered for a variety of intelligences and capacities?

- How does this activity allow students to practise more than one thing at a time?
- How does this activity require or encourage students to use what they have learned previously as they practise new strategies and deal with new concepts?
- How will my students demonstrate what they know in actual accomplishment? How will today's lesson move them toward that goal?
- What will I be monitoring or looking for in my students and their work?
- How will I track my assessment of the students?
- How will I use what I learn from my students' work today to inform what I plan to do tomorrow?
- How will the students leave this activity thinking about something in a new way or change in some way?
- How will the students be able to trace and offer proof positive of their own growth toward understanding and meeting the critical standards of the unit?

Acknowledgement

We thank the many teachers and students with whom we have worked over the years to integrate inquiry models of teaching and learning across the curriculum. We especially thank teachers involved in our various sites of the national demonstration project in content area literacy, teachers involved in the Maine and Boise State Writing Project fellows, teachers at Foothills School of Arts and Sciences and West Junior High School in Boise, the gifted teachers of Tasmania, Australia, and especially Josh Hale, Bea Futch, Ashley Duke, and Melissa Newell who devised the "How can freedom and security be balanced?" inquiry unit, from which we have drawn many examples.

We have tried to show how the many techniques that are widely used in schools can become much more powerful by being used in service of inquiry and big understandings. We have done our best to trace the provenance of these ideas, and will gladly correct any omissions in acknowledgement in the next reprint if they are brought to our attention.

We thank our families and colleagues for their support, and the editors at Rubicon for all of their help.

GLOSSARY

assessment, formative: Assessment which provides feedback to students about what they have achieved and still need to achieve; it also provides teachers with data about students that can inform what and how to teach subsequent lessons to insure student progress.

assessment, ongoing: The continual process of monitoring students' learning and providing students with clear responses that will push and nudge them along the continuum of understanding.

assessment, summative: Assessment that summarizes students' achievement over the course of a unit; it is often used to compare achievement across students or against various norms and standards.

claim: An assertion or thesis statement — something you want others to know, believe, or do.

cognitive apprenticeship: A teaching model that inducts students into thinking and doing the discipline more like an expert, moving step by step toward acting like a professional.

complex-implied relationship: Seeing patterns within a text /data set or across texts/data sets that are unarticulated.

community of practice: The group of practitioners in the world who make use of a particular set of disciplinary knowledge. Because they speak with the same language (or discourse of terms, ideas, and forms) and use the same problem-solving tools, such a community is often also known as a discourse community.

competence: The capacity to use tools to get something done. It includes the knowledge of how one is competent, and awareness of standards of competence and techniques for improving.

complex implied relationships: These are insights garnered from seeing an implied, unarticulated pattern and connection among details that are various and distant from one another in a text or data set. Sometimes these details are cast across related texts and data sets, such as various ones you might read in the context of an inquiry into a focused topic. Seeing, reasoning about, and interpreting these connections is called making a complex inference. Understanding of any topic requires seeing these kinds of complex connections. As David Perkins asserts: information is a line, but understanding is a network, i.e., understanding requires seeing all of the applied relationships within and across related data sets.

conceptual goals: Unit goals related to conceptual understandings that can be used as tools.

confidence: A can-do attitude; self-efficacy; a belief that one will succeed despite challenges.

correspondence concept: Moving through the continuum from novice to expert; when an activity or reading moves kids closer to having in their heads what experts have in their heads.

critical inquiry: Inquiring in such a way that adds data or new insights to a question.

critical question: Also known as an essential question, guiding question, or big question. It is a question that frames an unit inquiry or the curriculum as a contended issue or problem.

culminating project: A unit-ending student project that demonstrates mastery of all procedural and conceptual goals for the unit. A performance of understanding that requires students to use knowledge in new situations as they apply, reshape, extrapolate, and expand on what they already know.

data: Evidence that supports a claim or assertion.

differentiation: Also known as layering, multiple challenges, or addressing multiple zones of proximal developments (ZPDs) in the context of a common project.

discourse: In cognitive science and in critical theory, this term refers to a system of ideas or knowledge (for example, psychoanalysis, anthropology, cultural/literary studies), inscribed in a specific vocabulary. It legitimizes and conventionalizes knowledge, knowledge-making, problem-solving, and conversations within a disciplinary group.

discourse community: A phrase that links discourse (a concept describing all forms of communication that contribute to a particular, communal, and institutionalized way of thinking) and community, which refers to the people who use, and therefore help create, use, and further develop a particular discourse.

directed reading thinking activity (DRTA): A teaching technique that guides student attention and strategy use throughout the reading of a text or through a problem-solving act, by focusing attention on what must be done before, during, and after the reading or problem-solving.

enduring understanding: A disciplinary understanding to be achieved through inquiry that students can take forward, transfer, and use in their future work in the discipline and the world.

essential question: See *critical question*. Also known as guiding question.

flow: A total sense of engagement in the activity at hand, a sense that nothing else seems to matter.

forum: A drama discussion technique for discussing issues in role.

frontloading: The activating or building of background knowledge necessary to approaching a text or task.

gateway: The part of the throughline or instructional sequence that follows the frontloading and leads to the culminating project and student independence.

generative topic: A topic, issue, or theme that can be used as the basis of an essential question. Generative topics are of intense interest to experts and to students. They offer various perspectives, depth, multiple connections, and significance to the learners.

genre: A set of texts that are of the same type and that place the same kinds of demands on readers, e.g., argument of policy, classification, lyric poetry, satire, ironic monologue. See *text structure*.

graphic organizer: Visual means (graphs and charts) to dissect the meaning of concept, and represent what has been understood. A technique for data analysis and representation.

heuristic: From the Greek word *eureka* — a problem-solving scheme or repertoire for reading particular texts, solving a particular problem, etc. Steps in a process.

independence: The capacity to transfer and independently recognize the need to apply a strategy, and the ability to use this strategy on one's own in this new situation. This capacity signifies the achievement of a new zone of actual development, as the student has progressed through a zone of proximal development to achieve a new independent capacity.

inquiry: Teaching in which students are helped to know how to do things (read and write) while they achieve deep conceptual understanding. Inquiry includes a problem-orientation/essential question, choice within certain parameters, clear goals, ownership, challenging and complex problems, personal and social relevance, assistance as needed, opportunity to improve, problem-centred group activities, independent application of learned skills, and real-world application.

inquiry square: A heuristic for thinking through a reading, writing, or problem-solving task by delineating the declarative knowledge of substance and form, the procedural knowledge or substance and form required to successfully read or write a particular kind of text or solve a particular kind of problem, and knowledge of purpose and functional value.

jigsaw: A co-operative learning activity wherein students learn a concept in a group, then go individually to different groups to share what they have learned. A way of dispersing and distributing expertise. Regroup to share the information learned.

mentoring: Assisting students to achieve deep mastery of cognitive tools by gradually releasing responsibility for completing a task to them. Teacher does — students help and students do together — teacher helps are the two steps of mentoring. Second step in scaffolded instruction.

metacognition: The ability to think about thinking; a reflective process that requires students to consider and reflect upon their problem-solving strategies and cognitive steps.

modelling: The primary form of teaching — demonstrating how to use a cognitive tool in practice and making processes of learning visible and available to learners. Teacher does — students watch. The first step in scaffolding.

monitoring: The careful observation of students using cognitive tools in situations so that student tool use can be evaluated, and appropriate feedback for future use can be provided. The final step of scaffolded instruction that hopefully leads students directly into a new zone of actual development (ZAD).

motivation: The continuous impulse to engage, read, or learn.

multiple modalities: Development and/or expression of understanding through the use of multiple forms of representation, such as visual art, music, dramatic role play, or graphic organizer. Involves the transforming or trans-mediation of knowledge from one form to another, and the use of different modalities (ways of representing ideas) together in ways that converse and complement each other.

placehold: To keep track of evolving ideas and data by putting them in a form in which the data can be retrieved, and in which new patterns and relationships can be seen. Notes, graphic organizers, visual representations can serve as placeholding devices.

procedural: Strategic; wide-awake use of tools to get something done.

procedural goals: Unit goals related to strategic mastery of various processes such as reading, composing, learning, or problem-solving tools.

process analysis (PA): A tool of teacher reflection and teacher research. A PA answers these questions: What did you do? How did it go? What did you learn? What will you do differently next time? Inquiry process analysis (IPA) is a reflection on a lesson or an attempt to try a new inquiry tool. Peer-coaching process analysis (PPA) is reflection on a peer coaching session or discussion with a peer. Research process analysis (RPA) is reflection on use of a teacher research tool. Note: research in teacher development shows that teacher practice is most powerfully transformed when teachers 1) teach in an inquiry framework and continually experiment with new strategies, 2) have peer assistance and coaching, and 3) reflect on and research their own teaching — learning from students how these students best learn and are best taught. These processes can be very informal and when all are present, teacher improvement and development is enhanced.

protocols: Also known as think aloud, problem-solving process. A protocol is a template for navigating a procedure or task. Think aloud is a kind of online protocol that reports on how one is navigating a task or reading as it is being done. The reporting out of what one is noticing, thinking, and doing as one reads a text or engages in another kind of problem-solving procedure.

reservation: In argument, a counterclaim.

ritual structures: Repeated classroom schedules, events, or techniques that assist students to work together and use various tools in consistently more sophisticated ways. Having students write exit tickets each day with a quick record of what they learned of importance and what questions they have is an example of a ritual structure promoting reflection, feedback, and self-monitoring.

scaffolding: A temporary support system provided by the teacher or class structures and rituals until the student is sufficiently able to handle a concept alone. It typically consists of modelling, mentoring, and monitoring activities.

schema: A rich set of understandings around a particular topic.

self-efficacy: A person's belief in his or her capacity to organize, orchestrate, and execute all the tools needed to complete a task or manage a situation.

sequencing: Instruction that takes students from where they are to where they need to be to understand and perform that understanding. An interlocking process of scaffolds that assist students step by step to deeper understanding and mastery of appropriate tools.

simple implied relationships: These are insights garnered from seeing an implied, unarticulated pattern and connection among details that are close to one another in a text or data set. Seeing, reasoning about, and interpreting these connections is called making a simple inference.

situated cognition: Meaningful context; a context in which understanding and problem-solving repertoires are actually developed and used.

sociocultural psychology: The study of the social and cultural formation of mind.

socioculturalism: In cognitive science, the theory that all knowledge is developed, cultivated, and used in social and cultural contexts that influence the construction and use of that knowledge.

stamina: The willingness to begin tasks and the capacity to pace oneself, persevere, organize, and sustain effort through difficulties and over time.

strategy: Specific method to try to understand a text or solve a problem. Differentiated from skill because those who are strategic proceed with understanding of why, when, and how the strategy works and is used. Metacognitive awareness is involved.

symbolic representation interview (SRI): Also known as symbolic story representation or reading manipulative — a kind of text or story manipulative in which the content of a text and the processes used to comprehend and respond to it are demonstrated through found objects, cutouts, and other concrete devices. It can also be used to symbolically represent problem-solving process in math, science, etc. It is an excellent technique not only for teaching the processes of reading and problem-solving with specific texts and content, but also for conducting teacher research into student reading, or helping students research their own reading and problem-solving processes.

tableaux: A drama activity used to visually demonstrate (act out) the meaning of a text.

text features: Various methods used by an author to draw the reader's attention to particular elements, such as italic or bold type, title, caption, glossary, index, etc.

text structures: A genre or text structure that uses conventional combinations and organizational features to assist in meaning making, such as comparison-contrast, description, definition, extended definition, narrative, argument, classification, ironic monologue, satire, and lyric poem.

throughlines: The instruction that continuously and repeatedly pursues the central concepts and procedures/strategies that students must develop over the course of a unit to develop understanding of the topics.

tools, cognitive: In socioculturalism, tools are any concept or procedure that can be used to do something and get work done in ways consistent with expert problem-solving in a particular discipline or community of practice.

topical inquiry: Inquiry into established sets of information, operating on established data sets to see new connections and patterns. The prerequisite to critical inquiry, which creates new data and insights.

transactional: The interpenetration of reader (learner) and the text (data) to create a meaningful experience (learning).

transfer: The ability to take an understanding forward to a new situation and adapt or apply it usefully.

transformation of participation: The way to understanding — by having one's methods of participating in a real community of practice gradually transformed to become more and more like the practical participation of real experts.

understanding: Knowing the story behind the story. Knowing why experts believe what they do and how things work. Knowing how they came to their conclusions. Knowing what other alternatives exist. Knowing how to apply, perform, expand, define, offer alternative perspectives to what is understood.

warrant: Something that assures, attests to, or guarantees some event or result. An explanation of evidence, usually a general rule or principle about how things work.

zone of actual development (ZAD): The zone where students can do things unassisted.

zone of proximal development (ZPD): The level at which students can do things with assistance that they cannot do alone. This is the zone in which all learning occurs, according to sociocultural theorists.

REFERENCES

Appleman, D. 2000. *Critical Encounters in High School English: Teaching Literary Theory to Adolescents.* New York: Teachers College Press.

Bandura, A. 1986. *Social Foundations of Thought and Action: A Social Cognitive Theory.* Englewood Cliffs, NJ: Prentice-Hall.

Beck, C. and C. Kosnick. 2004. "The Starting Point: Constructivist Accounts of Learning" in *Teaching for Deep Understanding*, pp. 13-20. Toronto, ON: OISE/EFTO.

Beck, I. and M. McKeown. 2006. *Improving Comprehension With Questioning the Author*. New York: Scholastic.

Blythe, T. editor. 1998. *The Teaching for Understanding Guide*. San Francisco: Jossey-Bass.

Buehl, D. 2008. www.weac.org/news/2007-08/sept07/readingroom.htm retrieved May 15, 2008.

Christenbury, L., and P. Kelly. 1983. *Questioning: A Path to Critical Thinking*. Urbana, IL: ERIC Clearinghouse on Reading and Communication Skills and the National Council of Teachers of English.

Copeland, M. 2005. *Socratic Circles: Fostering Critical and Creative Thinking in Middle and High School.* Portland, ME: Stenhouse.

Daniels, Harvey. 2002. *Literature Circles: Voice and Choice in Book Clubs and Reading Groups*. Portland, ME: Stenhouse.

Dillon, J. T. 1983. "The Use of Questions in Educational Research" in *Educational Researcher*, 12(9):19–24.

Earl, L. 2003. *Assessment as Learning: Using Classroom Assessment to Maximize Student Learning*. Thousand Oaks, CA: Corwin Press.

Frayer, D. A., W.D. Frederick, and H. J. Klausmeier. 1969. "A Schema for Testing the Level of Concept Mastery" (working paper No. 16). Madison, WI: Wisconsin Research and Development Center for Cognitive Learning.

Freebody, P. 1992. "A Socio-Cultural Approach: Resourcing Four Roles as a Literacy Learner" in *Prevention of Reading Failure,* pp. 48-60. A. Watson and A. Badenhop (Eds.). Sydney: Ashton Scholastic.

Freebody, P., and A. Luke. 1990. "Literacies programs: Debates and demands in cultural context" in *Prospect: Australian Journal of TESOL,* 5(3):7-16.

Herber, H. 1978. *Teaching Reading in Content Areas,* Upper Saddle River, NJ: Prentice-Hall.

Lehrer, R. 1993. "Authors of knowledge: Patterns of hypermedia design." In S. P. Lajoie and S. J. Derry (Eds.). *Computers as Cognitive Tools*, pp.197-227. Hillsdale, NJ: Lawrence Erlbaum.

McKeown, M. G., I. L. Beck, and M. J. Worthy. 1993. "Grappling With Text Ideas: Questioning the Author" in *Reading Teacher*, 46(7):560-566.

Morgan, N. and J. Saxton. 2006. *Asking Better Questions* (Second Edition). Portland, ME: Stenhouse.

Morris, A. and N. Stewart-Dore. 1984. *Learning to Learn from Text: Effective Reading in Content Areas.* New South Wales: Addison-Wesley.

Murdoch, K. 1998. *Classroom Connections: Strategies for Integrated Learning*. Eleanor Curtain Publishing, South Yarra.

Pajares, F. 1996. "Self-Efficacy Beliefs in Academic Settings" in *Review of Educational Research*, 66(4):543–578.

Palincsar, A. S. and A. L. Brown. 1984. "Reciprocal Teaching of Comprehension-Fostering and Comprehension-Monitoring Activities" in *Cognition and Instruction*, 1(2), 117–175.

Raphael, T. 1986. "Teaching Question-Answer Relationships" revisited in *The Reading Teacher*, 39:516-523.

Ryan, K. and J. Cooper. 2004. *Those Who Can, Teach*. New York: Houghton Mifflin Company.

Smith, M. W. 1989. "Teaching the Interpretation of Irony in Poetry" in *Research in the Teaching of English,* 23(3):254-72.

Santa, M. S. 1988. *Content Reading Including Study Systems: Reading, Writing and Studying Across the Curriculum*. Dubuque, IA: Kendall/Hunt Publishing Company.

Smith, M. W. and J. D. Wilhelm. 2002. *Reading Don't Fix No Chevys: Literacy in the Lives of Young Men*. Portsmouth, NH: Heinemann.

Smith, M. W. and J. D. Wilhelm. 2006. *Going With the Flow: How to Engage Boys (and Girls) in Their Literacy Learning.* Portsmouth, NH: Heinemann.

Stuart, L. 2003. *Assessment in Practice: A View From the School.* Newton Lower Falls, MA: Teachers21, Inc.

Tomlinson, C. A., and S. D. Allan. 2000. *Leadership for Differentiating Schools and Classrooms*. Alexandria, VA: Association for Supervision and Curriculum Development.

Tomlinson, C. A et al. 2005. *The Parallel Curriculum in the Classroom, Book 2: Units for Application Across the Content Areas, K-12*. Thousand Oaks, CA: Corwin Press.

Vygotsky, L. S. 1978. *Mind in Society: The Development of Higher Psychological Processes,* Cambridge, MA: Harvard University Press.

White, B. 1995. "The Effects of Autobiographical Writing Before Reading Upon Students' Responses to Short Stories" in *The Journal of Educational Research*, 88:173-184.

Wiggins, G. and J. McTighe. 1998. *Understanding by Design*. Alexandria, VA.: Association for Supervision and Curriculum Development.

Wilhelm, J. D., T. Baker and J. Dube-Hackett. 2001. *Strategic Reading: Guiding the Lifelong Literacy of Adolescents.* Portsmouth, NH: Heinemann.

Wilhelm, J. D. 2001. *Improving Comprehension With Think Aloud Strategies.* New York: Scholastic.

Wilhelm, J. D. 2002. *Action Strategies for Deepening Comprehension*. New York: Scholastic.

Wilhelm, J. D. 2004. *Reading Is Seeing*, New York: Scholastic.

Wilhelm, J. D. 2007. *Engaging Readers and Writers With Inquiry*, New York: Scholastic.

Wilhelm, J. D., and P. Friedemann. 1998. *Hyperlearning: Where Projects, Inquiry, and Technology Meet.* York, ME: Stenhouse.

INDEX